Contents

HOW SOCIAL CHANGES INFLUENCE HUMAN SOCIAL NEED CHANGES

JOHN LOK

Preface

Introduction

What are the different unique characteristics between one developing country and one developed country ? How to judge whether the country had been either developed or had been developing ? What factors influence the country development speed? In my this book, I shall indicate New Zealand whether is one developed country or developing country, although its farming industry , e.g. sheep cloth manufacturing, breef and pork meat food export industries had developed long time, but what weaknesses, it owns to influence its continue development easily as well as what strengths it lacks to influence New Zealand is still staying in the developing stage in possible in global leading position. What factors influence US, UK their technological development can not be continued innovated to cause worse development to compare Germany 's heavy manufacturing industry future development in possible. In my this book cuntry development part, I shall concentrate on discussing these above countries' future development trend. Readers can have more clear judgement how they can develop more rapidly.

I shall explain why do our societies need to innovate? Product innovation, medical technology innovation, space technology innovation, transport service innovation, educational innovation. I shall concentrate on discuss these several aspects. If our societies can not be innovated on above several aspect, then what negative impact may bring to influence our societies. I shall attempt to indicate some evidences to explain what negative impact will cause if our future societies can not innovate to above several aspects in success. I hope my readers can make personal judgement whether my analysis and opinion is right or wrong as well as you can discuss your opinion to argue my view point after you read this book.

I shall indicate how our future transportation tool may be invented in order to improve our qualify of lives or standard of lives to be better. How to improve our future transport tools in order to avoid air pollution more serious? It is my this book discussion about how transport invention or improvement, it will influence public transport passenger service and comfortable need aim. I shall attempt to research how transport improvement question in order to let readers feel how it can influence future public transport tools passenger individual choosing any kinds of pubic transport tools need as well as how is our future actual transport improvement achievement aim in order to keep our standard of lives (quality of lives) can be improved to achieve the best service standard and avoid any kinds of future public transport tools passengers number reduces. Because any public transport needs to be improved in order to satisfy passengers comfortable needs. In passenger comfortable need psychology view, how to improve public transport service quality. It is my main discussion in this book topic, it concerns bus, ferry and rail public transport passenger psychology for example.

How social change influences human behavioral change ? Why human behavior may be influenced by social change? Our individual behavior whether can be influenced to bring negative or positive attitude by social change? I shall attempt to indicate cases to explain whether our individual behavior can be influenced to changed by social environment change. Readers can have more understand how and why social change may influence our behavior in possible. Behavioral economy is one useful and fun social subject. Behavioral economists ususally research how and why human behaviors may influence economy growth or recession, or how and why economy environment changing factor may influence human behavior changes.

In my this book, I shall attempt to explain how and why ecommerce may be one kind network human job. Also, I shall indicate reasons to explain why human network behavior may bring direct or indirect influences to economy growth or recession in our global societies in macro and micro economy view. Why leisure changing environment may influence human behavior , even economic environment changes. I shall indicate cases to explain any possible human social activities may bring direct or indirect influences to cause our social economic growth or recession in consequency in possible. I hope that my readers can feel more understanding whether what real meaning of behavioral economy is the relationship between our behaviors and our economy.

Prologue

Table of content

Why trip time reliability and crowding factors can influence MTR passenger choice.
What is the crowding difference
between train and MTR underground
train.
How MTR can attract many
passengers.

What the psychological need differences between rail and bus and ferry passengers

Reasons we need to improve public bus transport tool service quality p.36-43

What rail passengers really want rail innovation improvement

What ferry passengers service improvement need

- How can ferry service be improved affordable, reliable, convenient, flexible and clean will get drivers out of their cars ad onto environmentally responsible to passenger ferries?

Future Human Transport Need Change

How future our transport need change? p.44-50

What factors influence our future transport need change?

How transport has changed from past to present?

Future Non-Manual driving vehicle How Influences Public Transport Tool Passenger Need

Why and how non-manual driving car owners need raise public transport quality on travel time and fare aspects

How non human driving behavior can be influence by non-manual driving cars

pollution different policies implement will be needed to different countries in our future societies. p.66-70

- Future projections of air pollutant emissions
- Benefits of Reducing and Reusing policy
- How air pollution may influence the course of pandemics
- Ideas on How to Reduce and Reuse to implement

Improving internet technology development

- How internet can excite young to learn? p.71-75
- Internet can encourage Social Network Growth
- What Are Main Benefits of Internet Communication speed improvement ?
- Why does internet improvement can help any industries services or efficiencies improvment?
- Internet may become any organizational digital assets
- Internet improvement may assist robotic development
- Internet improvement to assist 5G laptop development
- How internet improvement influences AI provides medical service to hospitals ?
- The cyborg generation: Humans will partner more directly with technology when internet is popular to be used in any where
- Everyone agrees that the world will be putting AI to work, when internet is improvement to raise robotic efficiency and performance improvement
-

Discovery new health medicine drugs

- Why do we need drug discovery? p.76-80
- Where do new drugs come from? Why does it take so long to get a new drug approved? Why are drugs so expensive?

- China share market investing behavior

ONE

Future Developed Countries What Will Need To Innovate

Reasons Medical Technology Needs To Be Innovate

Medical technology improvement how brings medical equipment and medical health service performance improvement

Nowadays, our medical technology had been improving, patients can give excellent medical equipment and medical service to raise their health improvement ratio, human's life can be also prolong. Instead of medical technology improvement can help patients to improve health better aspect, whether medical technology can bring other benefits , such as social development, GDP growth, create job chance, improvement hospital service performance to let patients to feel more satisfactory these aspects.

This report is based on a 2018 Healthcare Analytics Summit presentation entitled, “Innovative Analytics: Using Analytics to Evaluate Emerging Technologies.”(January 23, 2019).It indicated that "U.S. healthcare spending alone is larger than the gross domestic product of most nations. Total health spending in the U.S. was $3.5 trillion in 2017 and is projected to grow by an average of 5.5 percent annually from 2017 to 2026. If all U.S. healthcare spending was separated into its own sovereign nation, it would constitute the fifth largest economy in the world. Much of those healthcare dollars is spent on the costs of cardiovascular disease, which surpassed both Alzheimer’s disease and diabetes with a cost of $318 billion in 2015. That number is projected to more than double to $749 billion in 2035. Additionally, consumers and providers are not experiencing a great return on investment in healthcare dollars. In fact, life expectancy in the U.S. does not compare favorably to other countries which spend less per capita on healthcare.

These skyrocketing costs have a big impact on consumers, with premiums increasing by 74 percent from 2007 to 2017. During that same period, employer contributions increased by an average of 48 percent. The impacts are also being felt by hospitals and providers. In 2016, 30 percent of all Medicare fee-for-service patients were part of alternative payment models; that number rose to 50 percent in 2018. As healthcare systems are squeezed in all directions, they need to determine how to cut costs and still provide high-quality care. To do so, they will need to look across the care continuum for answers, eliminate silos, reduce variation in

care, and look to emerging technologies."
Why does medical technology need to be innovate? There are two types of variation in healthcare: necessary and unnecessary. Necessary variation is deviation from standardized care based on individual patient characteristics resulting in improved outcomes. Unnecessary variation does not result in a benefit to the patient and instead increases cost. Variation in practice patterns has been studied in multiple conditions and the conclusion is that higher cost regions are not associated with improved quality or outcomes. While health systems have to look at variation in care in order to reduce unwanted variation, they can look within their own four walls to gain insights from data in order to reduce costs and improve care. So, if medical equipment technology can be innovated, it can bring cost reduces benefit to hospitals as well as patients can get more health benefit and they can also feel more satisfactory and comfortable feeling when they need to live in any one hospital room.

- How to Improve Outcomes and Decrease Costs for hospitals ?

Health systems have struggled to answer the question of how to improve outcomes and decrease costs. New solutions are needed to answer an old problem. Healthcare systems can focus on these four pillars of healthcare improvement, when medical technology can be innovated in success, it can bring these benefits to any hospitals in possible, they may include :
Population Health Management – Improve the health of the population through adherence to clinical guidelines across the continuum. Quantify the population needs and measure adherence to clinical guidelines.

Develop strategies and tools to improve care access and efficiency.

Reduce Clinical Variation – Transform care delivery through the reduction of clinical variation. Reduce unnecessary variation in clinical care.

Standardize care pathways and protocols.

Increase value.

Test New Processes of Care and Payment Models – Transform care delivery by piloting new and creative processes and payment models. Build on existing best practice programs and protocols to improve quality and efficiency in care delivery.

Develop and test new payment models.

Leverage Cutting Emerging Healthcare Technology – Explore new ways to efficiently care for patients. Implantable monitors.

Complex procedures and surgeries.

As emerging healthcare technology comes into greater focus, it's important for healthcare systems to evaluate the safety and effectiveness in order to effectively harness new technology for better care and reduced costs.

Optimizing Care Across the Cardiovascular Continuum

Additionally, in looking for the highest impact projects to tackle, health systems can look to optimize care across the cardiovascular continuum:

Primary Care – providers can emphasize a healthy lifestyle, use routine treatment protocols, and follow referral protocols.

Outpatient Cardiology – provide timely access to specialists, use guideline driven testing and treatment, and employ comprehensive diagnostic testing.

Sub-Specialty Care and Emergency Services – Standardize emergency care and protocols for complex patients

requiring further evaluation and treatment.
Advanced Therapies – Look at whether the right patients are receiving right complex procedures.
Thus, all of above medical expenditure cost reduces and medical service performance improvement may be caused when any hospital begins to attempt to spend some expenditure to get long term medical equipment life useful benefits fot their patients. It is one good behavioral economic benefit to any hospitals.

● Why medical equipment innovation can bring medical improvement ?

Medical innovations can have vastly improved the human condition. Our pharmaceutical, biotech, medical technology, device and diagnostics companies have helped people live longer, with less pain and greater quality of life. Over the past century, the life sciences has eradicated some of the world's most dreaded diseases such as polio and smallpox. More recently, the industry has made other diseases such as breast cancer, HIV/AIDS, heart disease and lung cancer no longer the death sentences that they once were.
What is Medical Innovation's Overlooked Benefit ? With these medical innovations, past and future, comes an often-overlooked benefit: the incalculable billions of dollars in savings to patients, their families, insurers, employers, governments and hospitals in avoided medical expenses associated with keeping people healthy or curing them of a life-long, chronic condition. Certainly, these medicines, therapies, medical technologies, devices and diagnostic tools keep people healthier. They limit the need for frequent visits to the doctor. They help to avoid costly hospital stays. They help patients avoid expensive surgeries.

Unfortunately, these tremendous cost savings often go unrecognized. Instead, we hear frequent reports about the high cost of medicine or about new technologies or diagnostic tools being deemed "too expensive" or "unnecessary." We hear that medical innovation is a cost-driver, not a cost-saver. Thus, when any hospitals' medical equipment can be innovated to bring more advaned surgeon equipment or any cancer patient, brain patient user facility. Consequently, in long term, I believe that it can help any hospitals to reduce long time medical equipment repairement expense, in economic benefit, it can help any hospitals to save cost to need to buy any new medical equipment when they are old or bad, if the hospitals can spend some extra expenditure to buy any new innovated medical equipment for their patients to use in long time. It means that spending less expenditure earn long time cost reducing benefit to the hospital, in economic benefit view, it is value to any hospitals to choose " spending less expenditure for medical equipment innovative expenditure.

The reality is quite to the contrary. Medications, therapies and medical technologies and devices not only save lives — they save money. By eradicating a disease, people no longer need to seek or spend money on treatment. By better managing and preventing more serious complications from an existing disease, people avoid more costly medical care. By discovering a new treatment or cure, the costs that would have been incurred in addressing a patient's ongoing medical issues can be avoided entirely. Therefore, developing new treatments, cures and health technologies is one of the most important steps we can take — not only to save lives and improve the quality of life, but also to avoid the expenditure of enormous amounts of health care dollars.

reference
Analytics and Outcomes Improvement, How to Evaluate Emerging Healthcare Technology With Innovative Analytics , From :https://www.healthcatalyst.com/insights/how-evaluate-emerging-healthcare-technology January 23, 2019

Medical technology improvement brings what social influences
How much savings does medical innovation produce? There is not one, simple answer to that question. However, there are numerous academic and government statistics that point to the economic benefits of innovation in the health-care marketplace. In a paper published by the Journal of Political Economy in 2006, it was estimated that over the preceding 50 years, medical innovation had been the source of nearly half of all economic growth in the United States. Impressively, for every dollar spent on innovative medicines, total healthcare spending is reduced by $7.20, according to an NBER paper. As for the price of medicine in America, only 9 cents of every health care dollar spent in America goes to medicines, according to the Centers for Medicare & Medicaid Services (CMS) in 2013. The other 91 cents goes to hospitals, physicians, clinics, long-term care facilities, and government administration and net cost of health insurance. Imagine if we could use that 9 cents to reduce the remaining 91 cents or even avoid significant portions of it in the first place. The result would be saved lives and even greater health-care savings. So, if medical innovation succeeds, then the country will reduce much medicine expense. It implies that medical innovation

can help many people reduce to spend medical expenditure, such as medicine expenditure is reduced because they can have more health. Whewn many people can have more health, our burden for medical expense will also be influenced to reduce. It is one good example of social medical expense reducing, when our medical technology improvement system is innovated in success.

However, healthCare Institute of New Jersey (HINJ) President and Chief Executive Officer Dean J. Paranicas Dec. 18, (2014) has authored the following op-ed on the life sciences and the value of medical innovation, he indicated that medication adherence also plays an important role in health-care savings, as medical innovations can provide no benefit if they are not accessed by patients. Of the approximately 187 million Americans who take one or more prescription drugs, it is estimated that up to one-half do not take their medications as prescribed. Poor medication adherence results in 33 to 69 percent of medication-related hospital admissions in the U.S., at a cost of roughly $100 billion per year. In total, non-adherence to prescribed medicines results in approximately $290 billion in unnecessary spending annually. Americans with chronic conditions account for 84 percent of health care spending. In 2011, this totaled more than $2 trillion. By using medical innovations to prevent or better manage the most common chronic diseases, the U.S. could decrease treatment costs by $218 billion per year and reduce the economic impact of disease by $1.1 trillion annually. For diabetes, the total costs of this chronic disease rose to $245 billion in 2012 from $174 billion in 2007. Without a cure, in the next 25 years, annual spending on diabetes is forecast to increase steeply to approximately $336 billion annually. For Alzheimer's disease, in the absence of disease-modifying treatments, the cumulative costs of care for people suffering with Alzheimer's from 2010 to 2050 are expected to exceed $20 trillion. A treatment breakthrough that only postpones the onset of Alzheimer's by as few as five years could result in annual Medicare savings of $33 billion in 2020 and climb to $283 billion by mid-century, while annual Medicaid savings could increase from $9 billion in 2020 to $79 billion in 2050. Hence, when US medical innovation succeeds, then it can reduce much diseases occur and medicine cost may be influenced to reduce because ther are not many patients need to buy medicine to eat in US drug market. Consequently, when drug cost reduces, e.g. US drug price is $100 for one kind of diseasem it may be influenced to reduce to $10 in US drug market. Then many US patients do not need to feel drug burden to buy expensive drug to eat when US medical technology can be innovated in success.

reference

New Brunswick, NJ— HealthCare Institute of New Jersey (HINJ) Dean J. Paranicas "the life sciences and the value of medical innovation. " December 18, 2014
https://hinj.org/the-value-of-medical-innovation-saving-lives-saving-money/

Medical technology improvement and GDP growth and job creation relationship

Can medical technology immprovement or medical innovation influence GDP growth? I beleive that medical innovation can help some countries GDP growth significantly. For India example, it is one high population ratio country, it must have many people need to get medical health service when they need to live in any one India hospital. So, India's medical health sector has high GDP income percentage to compare other industries sectors in

India. For COVID 19 disease example, it influences many India patients to give this kind of disease to cause they need to live in India hospitals nowadays. So, India must need to innovate its medical equipment or improve its medical equipment or medical health service performance in order to satisfy India COVID 19 disease patients their living hospitals needs in long time, it may be one year, even two years or more for this COVID 19 disease occurs.

Medical innovation is essential for sustainable growth and economic development. Several core conditions enable innovation and encourage economic growth. In the modern economy, innovation is crucial for value creation, growth and employment and innovation processes take

place at the enterprise, regional and national level. Innovation will lead to new businesses as well as to the increased competitiveness of existing enterprises. So, the country's any hospitals ' medical innovation will have indirect relatioship to help the country itself economy growth in possible.

Innovations represent a process, namely an activity of creating a

new product or service, new technologic process, new organization, or

enhancement of existing product or service, existing technologic process

and existing organization. According to the given definition, if we analyze its separate elements, we can say that we classify: innovations in production – development or enhancement of a specific product; innovations in services – offering new or enhancing of existing services; innovations in process – finding of new ways of organizing and combining inputs in the

process of production of specific products or services; and

innovations in management –creating new ways of organizing business resources. So, when one hospital or one country's overall medical system can be innovated in success, it will help the country or society to create a new medical drug or medical service improvement, new medical technologic innovative process, new hospital organizational medical service culture changing or enhancement of existing medical service performance or medical drug product manufacturing improvement to bring positive new medical innovation to impact the country's economy.

In economic benefit view, when the country has many hospitals feel need to change new medical equipment to replace their old medical equipment. Then, due to there are many hospital medical equipment buyers number increases or their medical equipment need number increases, then it will influence the country will have many medical equipment manufactures hope to manufacture different kinds of medical equipment to sell to themselves country's hospital organization buyers. So, it will influence the country's medical equipment market grows up. Consequently, this country's medical sector GDP growth ratio will be influenced to raise significantly. SO, such as India medical equipment market case, if COVID 19 disease still attacks to India itself country to cause many people feel disease. Then, it will influence many Indian need to live hospitals. Consequently, India will have many hospitals will need to buy many medical equipment to prepare for these Indian patients when they are contacting COVID 19 disease. In long term, India's medical equipment manufacturers ought need to prepare to increase medical equipment number to supply to India patients need when they are contracting COVID 19 disease. Finally, India's medical equipment demand number and supply number will begin to increase. It will create medical equipment job chance and any medical equipment manufacturers income will be influenced to increase when there are many India hospitals need to buy many medical equipment to prepare to supply to India COVID 19 disease patients to use in long time.

Wh Is The Innovation Economy?

To fully understand what the innovation economy is, it is important to first know how it came about. The theory of this form of economics was developed only in the last few decades. Previously, the growth of the economy was det

Is medical technology improvement essential to our future medical social service ?

Finally, I shall ask our societies whether we must need to improve our nowadays medical technology to be better in order to raise medical service performance improvement to satisfy global patients medical service care needs. To answer this question. We need to consider why our medical technology needs to be improve and what will be worse if future our global medical technology can not be improved in success.

I shall indicate COVID 19 disease occurrence case example, it is one good example to explain why our global medical societies need to be improved immediately. Nowadays, there are many health people become patients, even they die easily due to they do not know where they go out to contact this COVID 19 patients in indoor or outdoor natural environment factor. In fact, global COVID disease patients number is continue increasing. There are many COVID 19 disease patients need to live hospitals. If they can not get enough medical equipment when they are living in hospitals, then they can not prolong lives easily. Such as India and Afica , they are developing countries, when

COVID 19 disease had been coming to these both countries to cause many Indian and Afican get this COVID 19 disease to be die easily. In fact, these both coutries have many people are killed by COVID 19 disease. Even, developed countries, e.g. US , UK , there are many health people are killed by COVID disease.

I have no interest to discuss whether why and how COVID 19 disease can kill any health people to any countries. I have only interest to disease whether our global societies need to innovate our medical technology in order to save many health people lives. Nowadays, we facing COVID19 disease occurrence, it can cause many health people, old or young age people to die easily. In the future, we do not know whether there are another new kind of disease will come , even more than one new kind of disease will come. So, if we can not find new medical technological method to solve our nowadays old medical technology to be improved, then we will feel difficulty to solve future possible new disease occurs in possible.

ON conclusion, our global medical technological leaders need to sit down together to discuss how to improve our traditional old medical technology to be the best in order to attack future any unknown or new kinds of diseases occur in future any one day. If we do not have enough medical technology to prepare to attack any new kinds of diseases come , then we will have many health people to be killed by any one kind of serious diseases easily. So, it seems that medical technology improvement is essential because we need medical technology improvement to save our lives before any one kind of new disease comes to our societies. If it is too late to innovate our medical technology, then we may have many health people to become patients to be killed by any one kind of new disease in possible.

Technology hasTeTechnology has also made it possible for physicians and care managers to communicate with patients between doctor visits and after hKnowledge innovation how brings economic growth

What does knowledge innovation mean? Why and how do we need to continue to innovate our knowledge? Can knowledge innovation impact positive economic growth to our societies? In fact, when we can prepare to innovate our knowledge to be perfect. Consequently, it can help our social development more success, e.g. non manual driving vehicle, e-commerce, construction houses on water skill, hospital new robocit surgeon equipment, manufacturing robotic technology , even space touriusm leisure development etc. different kinds of technology innovation, they are depended on how human can attempt to learn to innovate or improve ourselves traditional old knowledge to be changed to any kinds of new or not discovered unique knowledge. So, human ought need to continue to learn how to innovate our old traditional knowledger to be more perfect. The question concerns how human can continue to change our old knowledge to innovate in succeed. I shall attempt to indicate factors to answer this question as below: What does knowledge innovation mean? The role of knowledge innovation means that knowledge management assists in building competencies required in the innovation process. Though knowledge accessibility and knowledge flow to organization, staff memebers are able to increase their skills levels and knowledge both formally and informally. An increase in skills can improve the quality of innovation as well as in society. When the country have many people can attempt to learn how to change and knowledge old knowledge to new knowledge, then they my bring their societies to develop more rapidly. So, it seems that knowledge innovation may help society, organization and individual to bring new knowledge to attribute to our future societies easily. It wil be a very important factor influence human future development in success.

However, knowlege innovation concept is not just represented by introducing or implementing new ideas or methods. The definition of meaning of innovation can be defined as a process, but involves multiple activities to uncover new ways to do things. Innovating helps developing original concepts and is to driver of optimizing operations. The purpose of innovation is to come up with new ideas and technologies that increase productivity and generate greater output with the same input on organizational aspect.

So, knowledge innovation may be applied on organization aspect, even individual and social aspects. On organizational knowledge innovation aspect, innovation secures tomorrow's revenue, lowers costs and differentiates companies from the market. However, a good business model that only provides a brief market advantage and disappears after a year is not the right approach. Hence, organizational knowledge innovation aims to help the organization to raise competitive effort in long term.

Does knowledge provide innovation in organizations? Knowledge managment creates a culture conductive to tacit knowledge creation, sharing ideas in the organization, which plays an important role in the innovation process. Is knowledge management ncecessary for innovation? Beside the financial basis knowledge is the most important resource for innovations, in order to lead a company successfully, systematic handling of " knowledge", becomes more important. Today, the increase in value develops from the productivity and the innovation in business society.

What is the role of knowledge for individual? Knowledge is important for personal growth and development, knowledge sharpens our skills like reasoning and problem solving. A strong base of knowledge helps brains function more smoothly and effectively. We become smarter with the power of knowledge and solve problems more easily. Hence, innovation is about knowledge creating new possibilities through combining different knowledge sets. These can be in the form of knowledge about what is technically possible or not particular configuration of this world meet an articulated or latent need.

For knowledge innovation can bring the positive effects of technology improvement example, there are just a few of the ways in which technology may positively affect our physical and mental health. Health apps to track chronic ilnesses and communicate vitual information to doctors , health apps that anyone tracks diet, any kinds of sport exercise and mental health information . Hence, technololgy innovation had been applied to health apps smart phone product to help we to track our health from ourselves smart phone apps equipment easily any time.

What impact did this innovation have on daily life? It increased the regional differences among various groups of people across the country, it become a major method of long distance commnication to many years. It allowed people to sign documents from across the country. So, innovation can be applied to administive tasks aspect. Also, it can increase productivity and brings citizens new and better goods and services that improves our overall standard of living.

The benefits of inovation are sometimes slow to materialize. They often fell broadly across the entire population. According to Krathwohl (2002), he indicated that knowledge can be categorized into four types: (1) factual knowledge (2) conceptual knowledge (3) procedural knowledge and (4) metacognitive knowledge. So, if human hopes to implement knowledge innovation in success, we need to know how to learn these 4 types of knowledge innovation elements. For organizational knowledge management components example, the best four components are people, process, content/ IT and strategy.

Regardless of the industry size or knowledge needs of your organizations, organizations always need people to lead, sponsor, and support knowledge sharing. Sharing knowledge innovation how influences social development. Social innovation includes social processes of innovation, such as open source methods and techniques and also the innovation which have a social purpose, like activism , virtual volunteering, or distance learning. Social innovation may include the social processes of innovation. However, social innovation is important because it can provide a unique opportunity to step back from a narrow way of thinking about social enterprise, business engagement and to recognize instead the interconnectedness of various factors and stakeholders. For science and technolgical social innovation example, science and technology can help a nation's process and development science and technology innovation are connected with development because they have hostorical record of bringing advances that have led to healthier, longer, weathler and more productive lives and they are key ingredients to solutions to the most serious poverty and economic development challenges.

So, social innovation may bring human benefits, such as providing food and lifestyle products world wide with focus on environmental and social innovation , giveing every child in the world the chance to learn code and helping the visually impaired interact with their surroundings. Hence, social innovation means new solutions (products, services, models, markets, processes etc.) that stimultaneously meet a social need (more effectively than existing solutions) and lead to new or improved capabilities and relationships and better use of assets and resources. However, a social innovation process consists of a sequence of activities that seals to find solutions to a special challenge. The process itself brings a new approach that has social impact in its means (process) and ends (solution).

There are 6 keys characteristics of a social innovation, as told by Colombian social enterprises, they include: Adresses real needs of people in a community, requires a deep understanding of the problem, localizes and humanizes the problem, builds trust and collaborates with the community in need, is sustainable and scalable and adapts constantly. Hence, every one may attempt to learn in social innovation. You will learn what social innovations are and understand how they are help solve societal problems. You will get an overview of important literature and debates on social innovation. You will also learn and apply methods to develop , implement and scale social innovations.

How can social innovation be improved? Major cross business/cross functional projects should also have social innovation objectives include: leadership programs that include volunteering activities may help employees develop their skills and lead to greater innovations during their daily work in any organizations. How does the idea of social innovation connect with social needs? We define social innovations as new approaches to addressing social needs. They are social in their means and in their ends. They engage and mobilize the beneficiaries and help the

transform social relations by improving beneficiaries' access to power and resources.
For social innovation on education aspect, teaching technological literacy, critical thinking and problem, solving through science education gives students the skills and knowledge, they need to succeed in school and beyond. The essence of how science and technology contributes to society in the creation of new knowledge , and then utilization of that knowledge to boost the prosperity of human lives, and to solve the various issues facing society.
On conclusion, social innovation may be future social knowledge innovation to help us to solve problems, it is an issue within the society that makes it difficult for people to achieve their full potential issue, e.g. poverty, unemployment, unequal opportunity, racism and mainutrition are examples of social problems , even housing shortagfe, employment discrimination and child abuse and neglect. Thus, as above evidences indication, they can explain why we must need to innovate our future knowledge in order to help us to solve any organizations, social and individuals challenges more easily.

Organization product and manufacturing process and workplace innovation

Why do businesses need to innovate their products to raise good quality, good design shape to attract custoimers consideration sometimes? What advantages will be bought to the businessmen after their products had been innovated in success? Can products innovation help the product to improve its market image? Can product innovation raise economy growth? I shall attempt to indicate reasons to explain above questions?
In our business societies, any products ought need to be concerned how to innovate them to be good quality. The

key practical benefits of innovation may include: Improved productivity, reduced cots, increased competitivenesss, improveed brand recognition and value, building new business partners relationship, helping the business to increase turnover and improved profitability.

So, it seems that product innovation may bring positive impact more than negative impact to any businesses. In fact, after the buysiness innovates itself products, innovation ought may help the business to charge higher prices for new products before competitors products come on the market. Being innovative good for the firm's reputation, even people naturally interested in its future products, if they have been first in the past as well as innovations in processes can add value to existing products/ services.

So, the meant is by product innovation, it means that a product innovation is the introduction of a good or service that is new or significantly improved with respect to its characteristics of intended uses. Maninly, these reasons can explain why innovation is important: Innovation grows business, increasing profit, innovation helps any businesses stay ahead of the competitiion, innovation helps businesses take advantage of new technologies.

On organizational benefit aspect from innovation, innovation may help organizations differentiate themselves , e.g. if your organization is using innovation on its processes, its because doing so will save your time, money, or other resources, and give your organization a competitive advantage over other companies stuck in their system.

In common, innovation may include four types. Incremental, disruptive , archihectural and radical, they help illustrate the various ways that companies can innovate. For technological innovative advantages, it increases productivity and brings citizens new and better goods and services that improve their goods and service that improve their overall standard of living.

The benefits of innovation are sometimes slow to materialize. They often broadly across the entire population. Hence, the advantage of product innovation may include: Growth, expansion and gaining a competitive advantage. A business that is capable of differentiating their product from other businesses in the same industry to large extent will be able to reap profit. Examples of product innovation in improved products involves introducing beter or more functionality to existing products, e.g. electric and gas lawn mower, GPs in car , battery car, non-manual driving auto car etc. So, product innovation is the creation, development and implementation, a new product, process and service, with the aim of improving efficiency, effectiveness or competitive advantages.

How does innovation help the economy? In fact, one of the major benefits of innovation is its contribution to economic growth. Simply put, innovation can lead to higher productivity, meaning that the same input generates a greater output. As productivity rises, more goods and services are producted. In other words, the economy grows. Instead of innovation on product aspect, innovation is also important in the workplace, it can help staffs to raise efficiency. Innovation is vital in the workplace, because it gives companies an edge in penetrating markets faster and provides a better connection to developing markets, which can lead to bigger opportunities, especially in rich countries or developed countries.

However, when an organization decides to implement innovation before it implements , it needs to concern these possible risks of innovation. Operational risk, e.g. failing to meet your quality, cost or scheduling requirements, commercial risk, e.g. failing to attract enough customers, financial risk,, e.g. investing in unsuccessful innovation projects. But, when the organization decides to implement any innovation, it may hope innovation how contribute to success. Especially as customers become more demanding. Entrepreneurs need an innovation to survive to boost your business productivity, growth and profitability more easily. IN simple, innovation may improve sales and customer relationship, reduce waste and costs boost your market position, improve employee relations. What does the right time to organizations make decisions to innovate ? When the firm discovers its customers use the product and they field praise and complaints. And they probably have ideas, however, that can be refined into a better product. Innovative companies make it clear they want ideas, that the door is open and there is always a friendly ear for changes, then they will start to come it. It may be right innovation time, when customers have any unique idea to concern the product after they use.

What is required to introduce innovation in an organization? To successfully implement innovation, you need to know exactly what makes an innovative organization as well as how it contributes to its growth. Our organizaitons also need to require an innovative culture where everyone is able to think independently . So, these reasons can explain why our organizations ought need to innovate, being bold in taking on the innovation challenge build people's readiness and receptivity to change, assisting people to resolve their unconscious biases and resistance to it, developing both customer intimacy and customer empathy. However, although innovation can bring positive impact in a business, but it is so difficult to implement because new ideas and initiative depend on the people who work for the organizations. It is a lot harder to achieve desired results. Innovation is not about optimizing gross margins , but about attempt how finding new ways to create more value for yourselves profit image to attract more customers consideration.

Innovation is difficult to implement, because no system, process, or industry knows how to change, more innovations are worth exploring for many. Technology for example, can be re-purposed into new innovative solutions provide your customers with new value. The challenge is that when it comes to disruptive innovation, it almost always involves " higher risk" compared to incremental changes and thus can not be managed the same way as regular business projects are managed.

Hence, maintaining quality and product improvement and process development often involves standardization, whereas innovation can rarely be standardized . Also, new innovationds can not be measured using the same metrics and value drivers as the existing products and services . To overcome this major barrier to innovation, companies should approach disruptive innovation differently compared to how they are used to approaching regular projects. This, any organizations need to understand that they may fail to innovate. In the beginning, innovation and most specifically disruptive kind, is inferior to the existing products and services on the market. Because product improvement takes a lot of time and requires multiple iterations, the value for the customer at this point is minimal , when distuptive innovation initally caters only to a small and not so profitable customer base, established organizations are focused on serving more demanding, high and customers using their existing value channels. This is where it typically has higher profit margins, which is why established companies with rational decision-making processes usually choose not to invest in disruptive initiatives in the easrly stages. The problem ocurs when incumbents attempt to apply new technologies to trheir existing value networks or refuse moving into new markets because they are seen as too small to drive growth goals or are simply perceived to have too low margins. So, for organizations that prioritize reaching scale through operational efficiency, it makes more sense to focus on growing the business through incremental means, such as invest in risky and uncertain innovations.

On conclusion, in reality, however, organizations need to do both simultaneously improve the core business and exploit new business opportunities . Hence, when any organizations decide to innovate their product, or manufacturing processing or workplace . They need to find a balance between different types of innovations to choose which is the most effective innovation, which is a lot more sustainable may be stay in the business and to grow it is the long term to in order to implement innovation in success aim.

Organizational technological innovaton

Which kinds of industries will be influenced by future (AI) technological development bring economy growth

What (AI) technological development will influence what kinds of UK and US industries development within ten years? Are environment and education and automatic manufacturing technologies will be UK and US future (AI) new technological development trends? What will be the difference between the (AI) developed countries and (non AI) developing countries future technologies development both in the future?

1 (AI) online teaching technology development

Future, (AI) online teaching method will be popular to be applied to teach to any university in possible, even secondary and primary schools. Because internet service is free charge to any students in any countries. Many different age students who can know how to apply internet as well as internet studying is very convenient to any students who can to internet to learn or study in home or public library or school library conveniently. Teachers do not need spend much time to teach students in classroom. They can use internet to teach teachers by face to face seeing and talking to their individual student from every student's computer. So, students do not also often spend much time to go to school to learn. So, developing any fast speed and time saving and talking and listening online teaching methods will be popular needs to any UK primary and secondary and university students in the future. It will be one new technological teaching method to change the traditional classroom educational method in UK and schools. For example, when one UK student who had left UK and is living in another country long time. If any UK school did not provide online teaching service to any UK students. It means that the UK citizen can not choose study himself/herself any UK school if who still hope to study any UK course when who is living in another country. Even one foreign student who does not go to UK to study, if he/she can find any UK primary or secondary or university to study from online. Then, the UK school won't lose one foreign student, due to it does not provide online teaching method to any foreign students. So, online Technology educational learning method will be one popular learning method which is enhanced, supported, mediated or assessed by the use of electronic media. Technology also enhanced learning may involve the use of new or established technology and/or the creation of new learning material. It may be deployed both locally and at a distance (i.e. a combination of traditional and e-learning approaches), to learning that is delivered entirely online. Online learning technology characteristics (features) include identification of a project lead for each area of any learning strategy, identification of two " quick win" for example lecture capture, electronic submission and feedback.

How can online technology enhance learning at UK any schools? It will include these several aspects to analyze. On identifying, prioritizing and innovation hand, online technology is a process for resourcing, prioritizing, acquiring and evaluating school software and hardware for UK any school needs. On staff development learning plan and a student skills development plan hand, UK schools need to establish a base-line policy on the standard (minimum) technology enhanced learning expectation for education each program and module and a mechanism for updating the schools' policies. On evaluation and research hand, a mechanism for engaging the owners of the technology enhanced learning strategy with best practice in the sector including contributing to and benefiting from pedagogical research and the evaluation of the student experience to UK any school.

Thus, UK schools can apply (AI) teachers to teach their students from online technological teaching channel to develop on educational aspect, such as (AI) teachers' digital literacies and appropriate technical skills that equip UK students for life-long learning, graduate level employment and professional practice, be empowered to learn how to learn with online teaching technology, using online technology to engage in interactive, creative and co-constructed learning with the potential for online learning in an interdisciplinary and international context, using online teaching technology to engage in learning with and from people from anywhere in the world, be supported on placement and in workplace learning through mobile applications and other supportive technologies that facilitate their online learning when away from the classroom, having access to innovative methods of online learning teaching and assessment that are the foundation of a research-lead academic environment, engaging with UK schools in developing , implementing and reviewing the technology enhanced learning strategy. Thus, in the future, it is important to build a capacity to apply (AI) teaching robots to teach their students from the online education technology to adopt future learning innovation and student individual online learning need (demand) to UK any school (AI) robotic online teaching trend.

There are many examples where UK academics working in isolation or in small UK teaching organizations or classroom learning groups have developed (AI) robotic teaching innovation that have a positive impact on UK students' academic experience , but these have remained isolated to particular modules or occasionally program. The aim of education researching online learning process is to identify the good (AI) robotic teachers' online teaching innovation that is being developed and to prioritize those that have the potential to make a significant contribution to improving the academic student experience at UK any schools. This online teaching process will need any UK schools which can plan how to apply limited resources necessary to achieve online teaching. In addition, the online teaching research process would evaluate and prioritize large scale educational software and hardware requests for primary, secondary and university students' requests. An important part to this process will be to ensure the integration of (AI) robotic teaching tools and their educational method to be applied to online educational products and packages that school staff and students regular use to make routine working and access as seamless as possible.

Decisions about school administrative online technologies should not be taken in isolation before assessing the impact on UK teaching staff. In addition, a range of techniques such as, (AI) robotic online expert facilitation, (AI) robotic coaching and peer support will be used to support individuals, groups or longer academic units, who are learning on major technology enhanced (AI) robotic teching online learning projects. Staff engagement may also facilitated through incorporating technology that is used in teaching staff research and/or professional activity that can be cooperated into their teaching.

Consequently, (AI) robotic online learning technology can develop UK students skills, UK schools need to understand how UK students understand technology and learn with it, therefore the digital literacy strategy needs to be considered as part of the overall strategy as well as the relevant skills development in UK employability strategy. So, in the future, (AI) teaching robotic online learning and teaching technology will make it clear that students will develop technical skills the appropriate level for graduate employability and professional practice. Also, in the future, the (AI) robotic teaching online technology can enhance learning working group to discuss external development, that are of educational strategic importance, understanding and evaluating current best practice and research and understanding and evaluating the online educational strategic contribution that pedagogical research and student feedback can have on online educational strategy, policy and practice. The (AI) robotic teaching e-learning unit is responsible for informing and educating. This could be done by, for example, providing a short digest of relevant information for each meeting and by setting aside a proportion of each school meeting to discuss a topic of particular (AI) robotic teachers to be applied to online educational strategic interest to every school. Academics that have not got a specialist interest in (AI) robotic teaching online educational technology enhanced learning will need relevant information at an appropriate time. This could be provided at a school department or faculty level and this will have clear links to the staff and (AI) robotic teaching online teaching development plan. Hence, future (AI) robotic teaching online educational development strategy will influence any UK or US educational school technological improvement in the future (AI) robotic online teaching method.

2 (AI) robotic environmental protection technology

Can future (AI) robotic environment technology be valid to human to develop? Nowadays, global air and water pollution is serious. For example, UK has many farming is polluted by the water and air pollution. It will influence UK farmers' income if whose farm land (natural resource) is polluted by water or air (natural resource). Even it will influence UK citizen will encounter food shortage if UK farmers can not grow any fresh and health food to provide the enough food numbers to eat every day. Moreover, air and water pollution will influence UK citizen drink the polluted water and breathe the dirty air to live every day.

This natural resource (air and water challenge) will influence UK citizen health to cause illness , even death every easily. So, UK government can not neglect the natural environment pollution challenge. The environmental protection technology will help the UK and development countries to solve the challenge of climate change to avoid or reduce farming, foods, or vegetable or fruits or rice, pork, livestock numbers loss threats, i.e. the development and deployment of low carbon energy technology, including technology for the efficient use of energy. The commercialization of low carbon energy and energy efficiency technologies in the UK, with a specific focus on the demonstration and deployment phases of bringing low carbon technologies to UK market.

The UK Government needs to deliver a low carbon economy and to meet UK ambitions emission reduction target. So, low carbon and environmental protection technology researching and development will reduce the carbon intensity of energy production as well as reduce energy demand, towards meeting the contributing UK's ambitions production as well as reduce energy demand, and renewable energy goals. The use of energy (including transportation fuel) and the UK's targets on climate change, for example, by helping the UK make a step change in increasing deployment of renewable energy, improving UK energy efficiency and helping low carbon technologies reach the market. The development of low carbon technologies, and to realize the benefits of doing so in terms ensuring security of energy supply for the UK future economy development.

In UK, private sector investment in technology innovation in the low carbon energy sector will other sectors of the economy. So, in UK energy technologies are likely needed to be developed to avoid dangerous climate change, or an acceptable cost. So, in the future, UK government will need to consider to research environment protection and low carbon energy technology. The activities will reduce carbon emissions, or have the potential to reduce carbon emissions on the longer term, through the use of energy technology will accelerate development and deployment of low-carbon energy and energy efficiency technologies will capacity in the demonstration and deployment of low carbon technologies. Innovation in the energy sector is the only way to identify, develop and reduce the costs of new and improved technologies for the extractions, generation, distribution and use of energy. It has long been an important means of achieving the UK's energy policy aims of a secure and affordable energy supply, as well as to develop the environmentally friendly technologies that are required in UK response to climate change, i.e. nuclear, wind or water, sun energy technology, which is future new energy technology is suitable to research to create to apply instead of current electricity energy.

How global warming influences UK agriculture growth. Scientists have also been fighting the use of chlorine in municipal water systems to kill various strands of bacteria. Chlorine reduces by about 80% the number of alimentary tract diseases relative to polluted, unchlorinated water. A relatively new genetically modified agricultural products. They were partly successful in Europe, such as UK (some countries banned genetically modified products) in spite of the fact that neither history nor research supports their case. People began to modify plants as early as the beginning of the agricultural revolution (8000 to 10,000 years ago), when they started seed selection and who have continued ever since. The green revolution of the 1960 year brought about strains of grans and rice more resistant to a variety of local conditions. The effects have been that countries like India, which had suffered from recurrent famines over the millennia, became self-sufficient in food due to the resultant sharp increase in agricultural productivity. It was a real science and technology over the poverty dominating most of human history. But it is precisely the products of science and technology that ecologists are so deathly afraid of. In an interesting study in a quarter (28%) of clinically analyzed cases of obsessive compulsive disorder were cases resulting from the fear of global warming.

To destroy the modern, whether industrial or postindustrial, civilization, human have to destroy an important engine of economic growth, that is its energy sources. And this is what eco-warriors try to achieve under the banner of against global warming. Thus, UK government will have responsibility to attempt to research new technology to fight global warming challenge for itself farmer benefits and even global benefits both on the future. Hence, future (AI) robotic development can be applied to environment protection aspect. Future (AI) robotic tools can help human to predict when and how any why environment pollution will occur in which countries and (AI) robotic tools can be one environment protection machine to gather environment pollution information to give opinions to human how we ought need to do in anywhere in order to avoid the places' environment pollution will become serious in influence our health. So, future (AI) robotic machince will be one predictive environmental pollution and bad climate change machine and it can give opinions to avoid serious environment pollution and give solutions to solve environment pollution any country.

(AI) will give global warming technological protection economic influence opinion to human

Some future economists indicated reasons to explain why UK government and businessmen needed to consider how to develop natural environment protection technology to avoid global warming challenge to influence UK economy development. They indicated the anthropogenic (human-made) global warming resulting from the increase in "greenhouse gas". They offered their perspectives on the scientific valid of anthropogenic global warming phenomenon, its probability of occur and expected consequences and is dominated by technologists, economists and political scientists, who considered the need to make the horribly costly adjustments in energy generation and usage suggested by climate alarmists.

Many stress that global warming is primarily caused by other phenomena than human use of fossil fuels or human activities in general. They are looking at the activities of the sun and impact of the larger universe as the main source of global warming and stress that global warmings (plural) happen intermittently with global cooling. I shall explain why global climate warming will influence to the political and economics of the issue to UK country. For it is the latter, rather than the global warming itself, that will pose a challenge to the Western world, such as UK and the world at large in the future. Scientists concerned who should move forward with policy measures to avert the alleged disaster. They also apply manufacturing theories to support enough to frighten politicians into action and scare societies into acceptance of measures that would sharply reduce UK citizen their living standards. Otherwise, UK politicians had support that bureaucracies were established, money allocated and lobbies created dependent on the new kind of subsidies. In consequences, climate alarmism and resultant interventions in national economies and human activities have become the increasingly wide spread and increasingly cost reality. With the growing availability of money distributed, and even more promised, a range of benefit of the global warming machinery has been on the increase. So, if UK government did not concern how to innovate new weather protection technology to avoid climate change adverse (poor) influence. It is possible that billions of dollars of UK public money are needed to spend on research global warming challenge because global warming will influence UK agricultural industry. UK agricultural industry is one important export income source to raise UK GDP income every year. If global warming become very serious to influence UK weather to be bad to cause UK farmers who can not grow good taste food and vegetable to supply to domestic and overseas food consumers to eat. Then, UK will loss much GDP income from local agricultural export sale. It seems global warming and agricultural production which has direct relationship to influence UK economy development in the future.

The main problem with climatology is that it must be based as already stressed on very many variables affecting climate and too few hard data necessity. Differences apply not only with respect to the scale of changes obtained, but even to their direction (rising or declining temperature). Some weather scientists indicated to concern global warming challenge. In consequence, it would be impossible to discover if and where errors were made not only in estimating relationships between variables but also in the quality of data used. (Hauser, J. Tellis, G. J; Griffin, A. 2006) They were comparing average temperatures measured some 30, 40 or 50 years ago by, say, 90 % weather stations in the countryside and 10 % stations in the cities with contemporary average temperatures measured by weather stations located today on 50:50 basis in the countryside and cities. Then, one could obtain the increasing temperatures without any real world climate or even weather changes. Comparability would be ensured if the same number of countryside-located and city-located weather stations had been compared for different periods. The alarmists intentionally mix up " temperature growth" with the trend of temperature growth. To give an example, if in the first decade the temperature grew by 0.5 % degree, in second decade it grew by 0.3 % and in third decade it grew by 0.1%, what was registered was a growth in the temperature, but certainly not a trend of growing temperature. A fourth decade should, on the basis of the trend, bring about no change in the temperature.

To conclude, scientists believed that global warming was caused by human's bad behavior more than natural environment influence. So, it is human's responsibility needs to solve this challenge, due to who feel earning profit aim is more important to protect natural environment, e.g. air and water pollution , due to manufacturing process is the main factor. So, UK has responsibility to attempt to research how to solve global warming challenge , such as it has many famous scientists who can devote their scientific skills to cooperate to solve global warming challenge with other countries' scientists. Some weather scientists also hypothesized that human may be at the end of the present warming period. If they are right, it would be bad for humanity, as warmer periods have always been associated with better conditions for economic activity. To sum up, scientists believed that global warming will influence human economic activity to be bad.

Future (AI) robotic environmental protection machine can give opinions to UK farmers:
Climate alarmists were able to convince a large part of the Western public and a majority of Western politicians of the cause of fighting against the global warming. It supposes itself in an instinctive preference for collectivist solutions in economic and social spheres, with negative to disastrous consequences when scientists are applied in practice, so UK government needs to concern global warming challenge, due to it is possible that it will influence UK natural environment weather to be poor to influence many UK farmers‘ agricultural and vegetable and fruit and rice wheat etc. food growth successfully. What is the global warming influence to cause disease? For example, ecological alarmists and activists (eco-warriors) never admit they are wrong, they long pursued their fear mongering campaign against chlorine. Their success in branding DDT a dangerous substance had a negative impact on the malaria eradication campaign in poorer parts of the world. Alternatives to be have been far less effective and the result has been the resurgence of malaria cases and the manifold increase in malaria -caused deaths to the largest extent in Africa.

3 (AI) robotic automation technology in manufacturing industry
Future, (AI) robotic automation technology can be applied to manufacturing industry. For example, nowadays, UK computer and space explore technology had reached the mature stage. It means that UK government ought not need to continue spend much resource to research these two kind technologies. Otherwise, the (AI)robotic automatic manufacturing technology, e.g. human intelligence new

product. It has need to develop because human intelligence machines will bring beneficial to satisfy human everyday life need, e.g. hospital patients' activities need, if the patent who can not walk easily, but the human intelligence machine can assist the patient walk to anywhere conveniently. So, he/she does not need to sit on wheel chair and apply the human intelligence machine man to help him/her to drive on the intelligence automatic driving vehicle to go to anywhere conveniently.

Otherwise, increased automation in low wage countries, e.g. China, Korea, Africa, Hong Kong etc. which have traditionally manufacturing firms, could use automatic technological manufacturing to bring lose cost advantage and potentially lose their ability of achieving rapid economy growth by shifting workers to factory jobs. So, UK government and businessmen needs to consider automation technology development, i.e. 3D printing manufacturing industry will encourage UK companies to move manufacturing process, closer to gain the biggest advantage from this 3D automation technology development.

A growing concern of premature de-industrialization in energy and developing countries could require new models and a need un-skillful the UK workforce. In the future, the best way toward for UK cities will reduce their exposure to automation is to boost their technological dynamic and attract more UK skilled workers. Automation technology progress can give UK manufacturers' employee benefits, such as long term healthy productivity improvement, raising productivity efficiency and product quality, macroeconomic and microeconomic effects of automation technological change, it's change will be beneficial to UK society, i.e. automation active labor market policies, which could help UK job seekers find jobs from training to incentive to support self-employment to create high technological job employment chance in UK society. So, raising science, technology, engineering and math subjects update skills level are needed to UK any universities, which can be increasingly important in UK society, these factors could complicate the ability of UK high automation technology education to adopt to the UK automation manufacturing technological change. A talent mismatch already exists in UK, with many well UK educated workers can find employment in lower-skilled jobs. To combat this, greater coordination will be needed between the education, training and employment sectors in UK society.

Why are high automatic technology product development models needed to research to UK any manufacturers? UK government and manufacturers need to consider how to achieve high technology product development models. According to Hauser et al. (2006) indicated the high technology (high tech.) development process, is influenced by the innovative process, bringing products on exception value which stimulate product market demand. Innovation provides products the specific basis for which world economies compete with each other on the global market. Able to find new solutions, innovations generate significant changes in existing markets, destroy them, or create new marketing (Hauser et al. 2006). So, UK manufacturers need to concern on any manufacturing high technology product development process because which can influence any new products development to manufacture to sell to any overseas or domestic both markets successfully.

What is high tech. product meaning? Mohr et al. (2010) argues that there are two reasons why it is important to clarify and specific high technology : (1) due to the impact of technologies on the economy, attempts are made to classify economic production and incomes ; (2) due to the impact of high tech. on the environment. Standard marketing strategies are being modified and adopted , therefore, it is necessary to know the products to focus on. Why UK manufacturers need to consider high technological product process. Nowadays, high tech. products are complex, advanced, requiring specific technical knowledge, which is technologically not discontinued and being produced at the companies which have twice as many technical personnel and invest twice as many in scientific research and development than other companies. Moreover, these products are time-sensitive as scientists are continuously searching for new approaches for invention of more advanced technologies which make all preceding ones lower-ranking. The most important, nowadays global consumers will adopt the particular technology. It means that global customers may delay adopting new high-tech. products and in order to mitigate the prolonged uncertainty require a high degree of education and information about the product and need post-purchase reassurance.

Anyway, nowadays customer individual needs in high tech. environments are characterized by sudden changes related to unpredictable fashion. Even, consumers concern about how to preserve new product' competitive technological standard is completely incompatible with technological uncertainty. The most important factor is the prevalence rate of any new products development process, which is influenced by slower than of traditional products. In many cases high-tech. automatic product market are being materialized slower than which are expected. The technological uncertainty challenges will exist in development process, such as uncertainty related to the timetable for development of the question whether the new product will be function as promised. In automatic high-tech. industries, the time requires for product development is difficult to predict as , commonly, it takes longer than expected , uncertainty related to unanticipated consequences and uncertainty about the product life cycle related to competition products. In conclusion, these factors will influence new automatic technology product development process unsuccessful, so UK manufacturers will need to concern on any high technological automatic product's manufacturing process.

Future economists predict automatic technology how to influence future UK economy

Before, all over the world presented picture of demonstrate in London on the occasion of the meeting of the G20. Some economists indicated disastrous economy consequences will occur to any one of Western country , such as UK, so if any one of Western country did not consider automatic technology development to itself country. They indicated one example, such as material incentives to produce disappeared throughout Russia and, when Society leadership called off the experiment, the country faced industrial output reduced to 10% of what had been registered in 1914 and agricultural output reduced to such low levels as to cause widespread famine.

Why would UK encounter disastrous economy consequences if UK government did not encourage manufacturers spend money to invest to innovate automatic technology industry? According to a variety of anthropological studies, a collectivity is unable to operate efficiently with everybody giving talent workers have chance to devote whose best effort to manufacture any high technological products, e.g. human intelligence vehicle or airplane. Hence, economic incentives are needed to UK manufacturers to invest high technological automatic industry development. Because the economists predict UK will have many talent worker numbers, their number will be more than a certain number of normal effort workers, due to UK technological education level is very excellent to provide to train many young technological manufacturing students to find this kind of high technological manufacturing job. So, the high technological manufacturing job seekers will increase and it won't decrease to UK job market in the future.

Assuming that UK high technological automatic manufacturing workers who would desire only to introduce changes in the workings of the international economic order and policies of countries participating in the present economic order rather than change the order itself, what will be UK manufacturers their specific economic preferences in the future? It implies tnat either concentrate on spending more investment to automatic high technological development, e.g. human intelligence automatic high technological products or still concentrate on spending more investment to common traditional technological products.

However, UK was a developed Western country which had had strong automatic high technological development effort very long time. Otherwise, it compared to some developing countries, such as Asian China, Hong Kong, Korea etc. Asian countries their future economic growth rate will show un- surprising , different patterns, so the Asian countries has weak effort to invest high automatic technological product development, such as human intelligence technological development. The catching-up process suggests low economic growth rate in the high automatic technological product development to the Asian developing countries in the future.

Hence, the future economists predict that it views as probable successors of the Western world economic leadership if any Western country , such as UK manufacturers who prefer to invest to any high automatic technological products development , e.g. developing on human intelligence automatic technological products more than traditional common technological products development. On the one side, but it seems important to stress that two very poor countries among the challengers-China and India-are examples of countries that changed their institutions and economic policies from no or little economic freedom to more economic freedom. Because there two countries whose governments prefer to lend loans to encourage their country manufacturers prefer to invest high automatic technological products manufacturing. On the other side, attitudes toward foreign direct investment (FDI) have undergone change since the 1960 s and a large majority of less developed countries, e.g. China and India are now competing strongly among themselves and with developed market economies for direct investment from multinational companies. So, UK will face China and India high automatic technological product competitors in the future. And in fact, all countries that joined Western developed economies did that without much (if any) external inflow of public resources. It is right time that UK government needs to lend loans to encourage domestic manufacturers to invest high automatic technological products to raise whose international high technological products sale effort to win its future competitors. So, machine resources will be increased demand to o UK manufacturers if who chose to spend machine resources to innovate to manufacture any new and high technological automatic products to raise human daily life needs in the future. It means that it is right time UK manufacturers need buy much machines to prepare to manufacture many future high technological automatic products when these machine prices are low. Because the future global machine prices will possible be raised if many China and India manufacturers will also buy many machines in the future. For example, USA government had provided much financial support to assist sugar cane producers to develop their businesses. And they are dependent to a much larger extent than sugar cane producers and sugar processors in the USA on government. Without very high subsidies to renewable energy generation, they would not have survived at all. So, USA government had been the first country which could lent much financial assistance to encourage domestic renewable energy generation manufacturers to develop high technological energy manufacturing business. So, UK government needs follow USA to lend financial assistance to encourage domestic high technological automatic industry development.

Future economists also predict China and India will be competitors for future leadership in the global economy, special high technological products. China has been the media and analyst's favorite for quite some time. Quantitative projections have seemingly supported such expectation. Such as China and India had manufactured many high technological new space rockets products, ocean war large ships etc. Moreover, China has become one of the major world trade players in the early twenty-first century. Many long-term forecasts, assuming similarly high economic growth rates in the decades ahead, predict that China will surpass the USA in terms of aggregate GDP somewhere between 2020 and 2030 or later, say between 2030 and 2050 year. The future economists conclude on the basis of these predictions that China will not only pass the USA in aggregate product (GDP), but its economy and economic policies will influence the rest of the world to a similar extent that the USA does at present.

I stressed a very important point, namely that the UK future high technological automatic product competitor China and India, namely that economies not only grow, but in the process change their structure. China and India have been industry very rapidly (the first transition) and building the physical infrastructure that accompanies industrialization changes to technology in the future. However, at a certain per capita GNP level the two countries, such as China and India will face another structural shift when which technological development will reach the mature stage in the future. China and India had been primarily historical pattern of economic development because the shift in the role of engine of growth from industry to services is to a much greater extent a qualitative shift. Both higher and different skills are required. And, even more importantly, interactions generating ideas driving the highly human-capital-intensive service economy require a much freer environment, not only in the economic area. Chinese exports have been heavily labor-intensive. This being the case, they contributed to the expansion of industrial employment, offering for the first time in the history of China a taste of (very modest) prosperity to more than 100 million new industrial workers and their families. This is the major component of the success accomplished by Chinese economic growth. Richer trade partners create room for more trade, so the Chinese should hope that intra-South trade, that is, trade between the emerging economies of Asia, the Middle East, Africa and Latin America, will open up new and growing opportunities. I presume that if Western economy , such as UK did not developed high technological automatic industry to stable their social welfare, so thoroughly slowed down their economic growth.

Will it allow China to accomplish the transition to a mature, innovation, service-sector-based market economy? It has allowed the economy to industrialize much more successfully, even if the labor shift from agriculture to industry has not yet been completed. But it is a long way off the next major test: the second high technological industry transition of the economic structure to China. Bear in mind that Russia attempted it twice and failed at both attempts.

But even, assuming that China at some point in the future does succeed in accomplishing the second transition, will it be able to supersede the USA, for example, as the main global high automatic technological innovation center if it wants to become the No.1 global high technological industry economy? Given the nature of the centralized state and its stability to collect financial resources , China's ability to increase research and development expenditure to high automatic technological products and to hire a mass of researchers, engineers, technicians and other specialists should not be doubted. This process in already taking place. But , again, Soviet Russia already exceed the USA in the R&D/GDP ratio in the 1970s, long before the communist collapse, with no effects on its innovativeness. Inputs matter less than outputs, quantity in the innovation process mean much less than quality. The latter characteristics depends importantly on economic, civic and even political institutions. Otherwise, independent India had three options open to it in 1946s. It could pursue spontaneous economic development, with some state intervention to be sure, along the lines of basically free market capitalism; it could turn the clock back and try to recreate the rural-agricultural and handicraft based. The dominant way of thinking was Society -style priority to industrialization and , within industralization , priority to heavy industry. In other words, not textiles and clothing, which has been developing well in India since the mid- nine teen century, but production of sewing machines and , even better, production of machines the produce sewing machines.

The results were only to be expected. The heavy stress on the expansion of capital-intensive heavy industries in a very poor country quickly strained the ability of the Indian economy to generate adequate savings. Moreover, some of these industries were above the level of industrial competence of an underdeveloped economy. Thus, the amount of required resources (capital, skilled labor) was usually larger per unit of output than in the same industries in more mature, richer industries economies. In another view point, India will develop light industries, just as any other poor country with a great deal of unskilled labor, had a comparative advantage and no less importantly, an economy in which, due to their low capital/labor ratio, light industries could employ many more people, spreading prosperity more widely in a poor country. So, it explain that why China will have more effort to develop heavy high technological industry in the future. Thus, India got less economic efficiency, less employment than in a spontaneously developing economy, less ability to compete internationally in light industries suitable for an underdeveloped economy and finally got heavy industry unable to compete even on the domestic market and, therefore requiring no less heavy a dose of protection. Overall India got an underperforming economy, in particular in its relations with the rest of the world.

To conclude by comparing the performance of the traditional sectors of the Indian economy and the performance of its modern, human -capital-intensive subsector of manufacturing and skill intensive service sector. The latter both employ workers with high-and medium -high skillful level (in branches ranging from computer software and biotechnology and pharmaceutical high technological light industry). India is ahead of China in terms of the output and export of such products and services. Thus, it implies that UK ought concentrate on developing high automatic heavy high technological industry, e.g. human intelligence technological products because these industry is not better development to other many countries' strong effort , such China and India large population countries.

Consequently, future (AI) robotic technology can be applied to medical service industry, e.g. in hospital and clinic environment to let patients to live in these places to feel more comfortable. It can also be applied to manufacturing industry to assist productivity performance rasing and computer software and biotechnology and pharmaceutical high technological light industry to improve computer technological software development and invention of much new biotechnology and pharmaceutical medicines for human health.

4 Increase development in genetics, human intelligence, robotics, nanotechnology, 3D printing and biotechnology technological industry

In US future, (AI) robotic tools will assist nanotechnology, 3D printing and biotechnology technological industry development, these kinds of jobs will be needed to increase development in genetics, human intelligence, robotics, nanotechnology, 3D printing and biotechnology. For example, smart systems homes, factories, farms grids or cities will help tackle problems ranging from supply chain management to climate change. The rise of US economy growth will allow US people to monetize everything from their empty house to their car in US. These new technological products development will change US patterns of consumption, production and employment adaption are also be changed by US corporations, US government and individuals.

Why will the technological revolution be broader socio-economic, geopolitical and demographic drivers of change to influence future US social economic and consumption pattern change? Future US most occupations will also be changed. When some traditional old jobs are threatened by redundancy and other new technological jobs will grow rapidly, existing jobs are also changed in the skill sets required to do them. The debate is between some economists foresee limitless new job opportunities and foresee massive dislocation of US jobs. In fact, the reality is highly specific to future US high technological production industry, region and high technological occupation in question as well as how US production workers can be raised themselves ability to actions the upgrade level of high technological production ability from various stakeholders to manage high technological production method change.

Overall, this is a modestly positive outlook of US high technological production employment across future most high technological production industries with jobs growth expected in several sectors. However, it is also clear that this need for more talent in certain job categories is accompanied by high skills instability across all job categories. Combined together, future US net job growth and skills instability result in most US businesses with face major recruitment challenges and talent shortages, a pattern already evident in the result and set to get worse over next five years in possible.

The question is how US businesses, government and individuals will react to these new technological job changes, due to talent shortage, mass unemployment and growing inequality challenges will encounter in future US society.

The current technological revolution does not need become a race between humans and machines , but rather an opportunity for work to truly become a channel through which US people recognize their potential. So, if US traditional low manufacturing skillful workers lack talent to learn new skills to prepare to do future new technological manufacturing jobs, such as 3 D printing, robotics, nanotechnology, biotechnological high technological products manufacturing jobs. Then, it will cause increasing of unemployment rate to some not talent US low manufacturing skillful workers. So, US government or high technological product industry employers need to consider this future unemployment challenge will be caused by high technological products manufacturing changing influences. It seems high technological development will cause these low manufacturing skillful workers unemployed rising numbers as well as high manufacturing skillful workers human capital shortage global challenges will exist.

In the future, the driver of changes to influence US demographic and socio-economic growth. They may include: changing work environments and flexible working arrangements. It means new technologies are enabling workplace innovations , such as remote working, co-working spaces and teleconferencing. Rising of the middle class in Asia markets. It means the world's economic center is shifting towards the Asia developing countries.
Some economists predict that Asia will be projected to account for 66% of the global middle class and for 59% of middle class consumption by 2030 year. In addition, climate change, natural resource will be constraints to a greener economy. It means that climate change is a major driver of innovation as organizations search for measures to help adjust to its effects. As global economic growth consumers are needed to lead to demand for natural resources and raw materials, over explanation implies higher extraction most and degradation ecosystem and these challenges will also impact US employment changes needs. All US government also needs to concern future global economic change influence. Hence , future (AI) robotic tools will assist these industries' technological development and creates more new jobs.

Artificial Intelligent

Social Military Defense Weapon

Although (AI) can influnence technological development to bring positive impact to bring beneficial welfare to provide human life. But, I also feel (AI) can bring new military to attack weak effort countries enemy from strong owning (AI) military defense wepon countries. If one day, some owning strong (AI) technological development countries' leaders who applied (AI) technology to manufacture social military defense weapon robots. Then, it will cause the third World war in possible. So, different countries' leaders need to consider (AI) invention ethic issue to keep world peace.

Nowadays, artificial intelligence (AI) is widely knowledge to be one kind of the dramatic technology. However, it is expected to continue, to have a disruptive impact on human's private and public life, so defense and security will be no exception. But how exactly will these be affected ? How will (AI) defense and security is incremental in nature?

To research why artificial intelligence (AI) has possible to be used to cause autonomous weapons by human. We need to understand these three aspects of relationship. They include cybersecurity and artificial intelligence and machine learning and autonomous weapon systems relationship between of them.

Firstly, we need to know what is the mean of artificial intelligence and cyber defense/offense? It means defense of critical networks: real time, pattern finding, anomaly seeking, it must utilize machine (AI) learning algorithms to efficiently, and instantaneously respond to potential network threats as well as it means human on or out of the loop. On the loop : it means anomaly detection: human notified, IT analysis, response. Out of the loop: it means anomaly detection: (AI) decides best method of response: quarantine, honey pot monitoring, hack-back. Thus, it is possible that (AI) can be used , such as autonomous cyber weapon.

What is artificial intelligence and autonomous weapons? Autonomous weapons mean one kind of weapon that can be selected and engaged a target, without intervention by a human operator. Are these machines artificially intelligent? I believe the answer is not, because present weapons systems are not capable of human level reasoning. But, (AI) algorithms are presently employed to process sensor data, monitor system health, take and respond to vocal commands manage data, navigate. This, future autonomous weapons systems will require stronger (AI) to be secure and operationally and cost effective. Moreover, self-aware autonomous cyber systems are crucial.

What is cybersecurity mean? It means the ability to control access to networked systems and the information they contain. It is acted to prevent , detect, recover, react. It is application objects concern people, process, technology and it's application goals are confidentiality, integrity and popular availability. Thus, what is cyber weapon mean? Walware means viruses, Trojans, zero-days, worms ransomware, spyware etc. Does it require a particular objective? E.g. military paramilitary or intelligence. Does it require physical harm? E.g. functional harm or interruption? Mental harm? Is (AI) a technological weapon that it is an object or tool? What about when it is an weapon agent?

In simplicity, (AI) can be one of scientific weapons platform. When one day, it is invented to be applied to control war planes to fly to any countries to attack enemies or it is invented to be seemed to human to replace soldiers to bring guns or any weapons go to other countries to attack. So, it is possible that future any war defense planes, (AI) technological automatic control weapon can be replaced of human soldiers or war plane pilots to control any war defense planes to go to different enemy countries to attack them easily. It is very horror matter to threaten global human's ourselves life in the future , if (AI) automatic control war defense planes or (AI) automatic control machine soldiers were invented successfully.

Hence , when (AI) can be applied to weapons platforms, it structures that launch weapons, i.e. jets, ships, vehicles. (AI) platform and weapon and software architecture components are be done one (AI) technological weapons systems. Thus, human will encounter any (AI) benefits or risks (threats) causes in the same time as soon as possible. If we can predict when (AI) weapon system will be manufactured or invented successfully. Then, we can reduce (AI) weapon systems risks , if we can threaten any (AI) scientists continue to invent any undiscovered (AI) weapons in any time to avoid the future first time (AI) weapon war occurrence in possible.

The (AI) weapon system risk means autonomy: the ability to problem solve technological war , when (AI) weapon system is manufactured successfully, the power to act, how to damage the (AI) weapon system. The power to chance to stop (AI) weapon system manufacturing processes, ability to create a new goals, how to change the (AI) weapon system inventors' or scientists' minds to avoid to apply (AI) tools to achieve attack goals to change to another positive goal. Due to human can't know a prior what an autonomous (AI) weapon system will do.

Although, human is known what (AI) is , but human is also known when (AI) scientists whose emergent behaviors will do to change to do any negative behaviors from positive behaviors. Whatever (AI) weapon system design we use, there will be cybersecurity, problems arising from computation design/complexity. Due to any one (AI) scientist can manipulate the system to act against itself, or who can utilize traditional " cyber weapons" against the (AI) weapon system, or who can manipulate the system to lie to humans, but also due to complexity, there is no way to know if it is lying or not or bounded rationality : satisficing.

Finally, the most serious (AI) technological invention risks are human is unknown these aspects of (AI) absolutely: They are not simple automatic systems, learning reasoning, communication of " self-aware" systems. Thus, human will face (AI) technological invention risks or threats. We need to find any methods to avoid (AI) weapon system is manufactured successfully to avoid (AI) technological war can occur in future anyone day.

1 (AI) system immoral intention

Why (AI) system can be invented to damage our society ? IS it possible to achieve this (AI) damage system successfully? ON (AI) attribution hand, it can be applied to cars, aircraft, which are subject to regulation designed to protect the public from harm and ensure fairness in economic competition. Thus, (AI) safety issue is important to scientists to consider.

IN general, the approach to regulation of (AI)-enabled products protect public safety issue should be informed by assessment of the aspects of risk that the addition of (AI) way reduce any respects of risk that it may increase. Also, where regulatory responses to the addition of (AI) threaten to increase the cost of compliance, or slow the development or adoption of beneficial innovations, policymakers should consider how those responses could be adjusted to lower costs and barriers to innovation without adversely impacting safety or market fairness.

For example, regulatory challenges that (AI) enabled present are found in the cases of automated vehicles. (AI)s, such as self-driving cars and (AI)-equipped unmanned aircraft systems. IN the long run, self-driving cars will likely save many lives by reducing driver error and increasing personal mobility, it will offer many economic benefits. Thus, public safety must be protected as these technologies are tested and begin to mature. Creating safe spaces and test beds for experimentation , and working with industry and civil society to evolve performance based regulations that will enable more uses as evidence of safe operation accumulates. Thus, it implies that any scientists can also invent (AI) system to control weapon defense planes or (AI) automatic machine human to do any soldier's behaviors to attack to any countries easily, instead of none driver automatic control vehicle invention. Thus, (AI) system can be applied to harm to human or achieve to damage our society aim by ourselves in possible.

The rapid growth of (AI) has dramatically increased the need for people with relevant skills to support and advance the field. AN (AI) –enables would demand a data literate citizenry that is able to read, use, interpret and communicate about data and participate in policy debates about matters affected by (AI). Thus, if (AI) technology is applied to assist human's social development and raising life enjoyment or benefits. It will bring positive impact to influence human's future life. Otherwise, if (AI) technology is unsafe to be applied to threaten human's society. It will bring negative impact to influence human's future life. Thus, (AI) scientists need to consider how to apply (AI) technology.

As (AI) technologies move toward deployment, technical expects, policy analysts and ethicists have raised concerns about unintended, consequences of adoption. Use one (AI) to make consequential decisions about people, often replacing decisions made by human –driven bureaucratic processes, leads to concerns about how to ensure justice, fairness, and accountability, the same concerns of human's safety issue. Thus,)AI) expects have cautioned that there are challenges in trying to understand and predict the behaviors of advanced (AI) systems.

Use of (AI) to control physical-world equipment leads to concerns about safety, especially as systems are exposed to the full complexity of human environment. A major challenge in (AI) safety is building systems that can safety transition from the closed world of the laboratory into the outside open world, when unpredictable things can happen. Adapting to unforeseen situations are difficult necessary for safe operation. Experience in building other types of safety artificial systems and, such as aircraft, power plants, bridges and vehicles has much to teach (AI) practitioners about verification and validation, how to build a safety case for a technology, how to manage risks, and how to communicate with stakeholders about risk. The risk means the harm of human's safety of (AI) damage system control machine invention. Thus, any (AI) scientists need consider moral responsibility when who decide to invent what kind of (AI) system machine to aim to bring human's benefits or attribute to human's welfare intention.

Thus, (AI) products safe invention matter will need any scientists' considerations. Because , if (AI) any products are unsafe or harm human's invention in the manufacturing process, it will bring any human's life danger when the (AI) system damage tools are invented successfully and are provided weapons to humans to use to attack other countries easily. It will cause future global human (AI) technological war occurrence.

I shall recommend the solution is necessary of ethical training for (AI) practitioners and students. Ideally, every student learning (AI) , computer science, or data science would be exposed to curriculum and discussion on related ethics and security topics. However, ethics alone is not sufficient. Ethics can help practitioners understand their responsibilities to all stakeholders, but ethical training should be methods for deciding good intentions into practice by doing the technical work needed to prevent unacceptable or immoral (AI) invention outcomes.

Hence, global human needs to concern (AI) weapon system invention security issue. Nowadays, (AI) has important application is increasing role for both defensive and offensive cyber measures. Currently, designing and operating secure systems requires significant time and attention from experts.

Challenges issues are raised by the potential use of (AI) in weapon systems. The United States has incorporated autonomy in certain weapon systems for decades, allowing for greater precision in the use of weapons and safer, more humane military operations. Nonetheless, direct human control of weapon systems involves some risks and can raise legal and ethical questions concern (AI) manufacturing process intention.

The key to incorporating autonomous and semi-autonomous weapon system into American defense planning is to ensure that U.S. Government entities are always acting in accordance with international humanitarian law, taking appropriate steps to control , to develop standards related to the development and use of such weapon systems. The United States has activity participated in ongoing international discussion on Lethal autonomous weapon systems and anticipates continued robust international discussion of those potential weapons systems. Thus, (AI) scientists have responsibilities to manage the potential to be a major driver of economic growth and social progress only, their (AI) intentions are not the global dominance aims absolutely, if (AI) product industry , civil society, government and the public work together to support (AI) positive development of the technology with thoughtful attention to its potential and to managing its invention threat risks to avoid (AI) products to manufacture to be used weapon tools.

Finally, I recommend that as the technology of (AI) continues to develop, practitioners must ensure that (AI) enables systems are governable, that what their inventions need to be openness to let public to know clearly and understandable; that they can work effectively with people and that their operation will remain consistent with human values and aspirations. Researchers and practitioners have increased their attention to these challenges , and should continue to focus on their future any (AI) inventions.

Hence, (AI) safe system ought to be applied to solve the biggest challenges that society faces, such as mobility for the elderly and those with disabilities, smart buildings may save energy and reduce carbon emissions, precision medicine may extend life and increase quality of life, smarter government may solve citizens more quickly and precisely., better protect those at any immoral invention risk and save money.

Moreover, (AI) enhanced education may help teachers give every child on education that opens doors to a secure and fulfilling life. Thus, these are the future human's potential benefits if the (AI) technology is developed to its benefits and scientists ought avoid to manufacture (AI) tools to cause weapon risks and challenges.

Consequently, the main point is that how experts invent (AI) systems. (AI) systems ought not be advanced weapon systems, it doesn't seem to be thought similar human soldiers mind and behaviors. (AI) system ought be systems that think like humans. (e.g. cognitive architectures and neural networks), systems that act like humans (e.g. pass the test via natural language process, knowledge representation, automated reasoning, and learning), systems that think rationally , e.g. logic solvers, inference and optimization and systems that act rationally e.g. intelligence software agents and embodies robots that achieve goals via perception, planning reasoning, learning , communicating, decision-making and acting function.

In conclusion, it is horror (AI) scientists will invent (AI) systems to be owned human's (soldier's) mind and attack strategic behavior to attack other countries easily, who must need to consider (AI) system ought be invented to own scientists' creating mind and non manual assistance functions for positive attribution to human's society. I expect that (AI) system can only be invented to create human's welfare in our future.

2 (AI) soldier weapon ethical, social and
economic negative impact

In the future, how human can avoid (AI) technological ethical, social and economic negative impact. Scientists need to concern these questions: how to develop of a good (AI) society, how the role and responsibility of the government, the private sector, and the reserch community(including education), in pursuing such a development, whether how the recommendation to support , such a (AI) system development may be in need of improvement.

However, none appers to deliver a comprehensive explicit vision of the role that (AI) system should play in mature information societies. Thus, (AI) 's potential contribution to social good shoud include an in-depth plan for linking in a comprehensive socio-political design questions of responsibility of the different stakeholders, of cooperation between them and of sharable values to understand of a good (AI) positive impact society, not a bad (AI) negative impact society.

Thus, the notion of mature information societies is introduced to stree the importance of addressing the current ethical challenges that (AI) poses in a comprehensive fashion.

It seems (AI) wil invention will be human's moral societal consideration issue. It concerns our (AI) scientists' moral issue, how who invent (AI) system to apply to which kind aspects. IF (AI) system was one direction on war weapon tools to similar to soldier's personal mind or attacking behavior. Then, it will bring poor social safety and poor economy growth our world, due to (AI) scientists' moral is low level.

Thus, the developed country US (AI) technological leader needs to focuse on the impacts of (AI)-driven customatin on the US job market and economy. It represents three specific policy responses to the perceived impact of (AI) on the US economy. They include these three aspects such as: How to invest in and develop (AI) for its many benefits, how to educate and train Americans for the jobs of the future and how to aid workers in the transition and empower workers to ensure broadly shared growth.

The future of (AI) influenced cyber conflicts need more than just the application of current and past solutions in order to ensure security and stability of societies, and avoid risks of escalation. To achieve this end, efforts to regulate cyber conflicts require an in-depth understanding of this new phenomenon, identify the changes brought about by cyber conflicts and the information revoluation, and defines a set of shared values that will guide the stakeholders operating to avoid the international (AI) war occurrence. This becomes clear when considering for example, cyber deterrence. Deploying conventional (cold war) strategies to deter (AI)-influenced cyber conflicts proves highly problematic and the urgent need to foster and coordinate new solutions able to account for the any kinds of conflicts of the cyber demain and of mature information societies to avoid (AI) technological war occurrence in the future.

We hope that in the on-going international conversations and reviews, the US government with further specify how " (AI) system invention law" fit into their vision of the future of society in this case the future of (AI) technological war and conflicts. Hence, (AI) scientists need to concern ethical issues related to (AI), like fairness, accountability and social justice can be addressed through increasing needs. Such as: how the creation of a new body focused on robotics and related (AI) system development to avoid to intent to apply weapon tools to provide advice on the policy, legl and consumer protection issues arising in these fields should be considered.

How to achieve ethical training of (AI) staff and ethical education of the public is certainly important responsibility for (AI) tools ethical behavior and design to the private sector and the citizens : of unique challenges that (AI) brings to society in terms in fairness, social equity and accountability are addresses. Thus, the development of the

(AI) technology and defining good (AI) remains problematic. In particular, the US government's innovation driven approach to defining the potential, positive impact of (AI) shows that more could be done to ensure that the opportunities and advantages brought about by (AI) are shared by all society.

An initial on Robotics, based upon the ethical framework and guiding principles is proposed. It should be complementary to legislaton and comprise ethical codes of conduct for Robotics researchers and designers, codes for research ethics committees as well as licenses (rights and duties) for designers and users. Thus, (AI) robotics invention of safety issues is very important considertion to any (AI) inventions or researchers. Every country's government ought have legal guiding to control their robotics' manufacturing intention. If their robotics (AI) is applied to seem to be soldiers to attack other countries to threaten their people's safety. Then, those (AI) inventors or researchers need to be punished by law.

In conclusion, I believe (AI) technology will be applied to weapon, when it's technological development is nearly mature to able to learn human's mind to do any behavior. During (AI) technology reachs thie mature stage, I predict the (AI) weapon tool , e.g. (AI) soldiers will have chance to be caused. This (AI) invention mature stage has these characteristics such as:

When (AI) invetion reachs this mature stage, computers and robots will develop conscious, intelligent, personified minds. Further, information technology devices and (AI) systems will be implanted into humans, enhancing, psychological and behavioral abilities and allowing for direct communication with artificial intelligent minds.

There will be both artificial intelligence (AI) and intelligence amplification (AI) in the relatively near future stage.

During the (AI) invention reachs this mature stage, these will be an ongoing mulit-faceted integration of information technologies and human life. Humans and information technology will cooperate. Humans will increasingly immerse their lives and minds in (AI) systems of technological intelligence and virtual reality. The distinction between humanity and technology will increasingly close dependence.

During the (AI) invention mature stage reachs that the environment will be infused with information technology, becoming animated, communicative and more intelligent. The destinction between the artificial and the natural will increasing close dependence.

During the (AI) invention mature stage will expand through virtual reality, simulated and virtual reality will increasingly into normal reality, e.g. the (AI) weapons is virtual reality to seem to be soldier weapon.

Finally, during the (AI) invention mature stage is as the global expression of the evolving human-technology integration a " world brain" and " world mind" will emerge on the earth. This psychophysical (AI) weapon system will enhance and enrich the capacities of both individual and collective cogniton. This (AI) weapon system is a potential starting point toward the evolution of a cosmic brain and cosmic mind.

Thus, it is possible that the workship raw data was a unique way in which (AI) could be weaponized to cause war, during the (AI) invention stage reachs the invention mature stage. However, (AI) weapon manufacturing factory will be built possibly. In the future, how will we defins and locate (AI) weapon factories. Especially, as these factories are no longer solely buildings , but a mil of virtual and substantially different facilities, particularly as it shifts from a physical assemly and development model to a distributed and flexible network. Needing minimal raw materials to develop (AI) weapons, the phsysical location of their (AI) factories could be anywhere and their identification from the outside, nearly impossible. Given the expanding uses for intelligent and super-intelligent (AI). How will we tell the different form a location that is manufacturing (AI) for the creation of weapons versus creating (AI) for an innovative new gaming platform?

In conclusion, human needs to consider every (AI) scientist's personal ethical or moral mind and research intention and (AI) system invention of (AI) weapon factories cause. During (AI) invention reachs the mature stage if human expects to avoid (AI) technological war occurrence in future one day. The technological development on autonomous military robots, ideally among relevant social groups and actors including human-rights, activists, researchers developers, engineers, philosophers, policy-makers, military authorities, lawyers, journalists and the publis need to consider when human has effort to invent autonomous military robots successfully in the future one day. Finally, some ambitious countries or dominant global countries must like to apply (AI) autonomous military robots to be machine soldiers more than human soldiers if (AI) technology had reached the mature stage. So, future (AI) autonomous military robots will be the next choice of weapon to follow nuclear weapon. If civilians were used as a human (AI) soldiers, the weapon simply ignored them and targeted anyway. This scenario highlighted the dangers of proliferation and quick replication of autonomous weapons. Unlike nuclear weapon, a piece of code for (AI) artificial intelligent soldier could be obtained on the black market and replicated at little cost and the hardware for this type of weapon doesn't require costly or hard to obtain components and materials. Thus, (AI) artificial intelligent soldiers can be manufactured many at cheaper cost. Otherwise, manufacturing one nuclear bomb weapon will spend too much cost. Hence , it is possible that (AI) artificial intelligent soldier will be future new technological weapon to follow nuclear bomb weapon. Hence, any country government needs to legislate to control any (AI) scientists' inventions whether they are attributed benefits or welfares to human or damage human's safety.

(AI) assist future computer
industry new gender innovation development

Why China's computer manufacturing and product development industry will be global leader to compete US computer dominant market. The reason is because that China will have possible to dominate global computer industry development if it can invent new (AI) learning tool to assist global computer systems to raise more efficient performance effort.

Nowadays, China's computer industry is the largetest hardware producer production and experts is dominated by Taiwanese firms. It is also the second largest personal computer (pc) market and domestic pc companies are top three sellers in global computer manufacturing and product development market. Forx example, Lenovo buys BM pc business in 2004 year. It implies US, IBM pc manufacturing leader can not dominate global computer market in possible in the future.

Reed Electronic Research, Yearbook Of World Electronic Data (2003) indicated that the leading computer producing countries of hardware production in US $millions and share share of total gogal production: The world region US was the global rank number one. In 1995 year, US had US $76,284 value, market value 26.5%. Then in 2000 year, US had increased up to US $ 90, 430 value, market share 24%. Till to 2003 year, US had fallen down to US $ 69,102 value, market share 21.7%. However, US hardware production was still the global rank number one , although its hardware production value had been falling down. But, the following second rank country, Japan and the third rank country, Singapore and the fourth rank country, Taiwan and the fifth rank county China which hardware production value could not exceed US till to 2003 year. However, although China had the lowest hardware production value US $5,600 to compare to among of these countries in 1995 year, but China had increased the value to US $65,000 and market share to 20.5%. Otherwise, Japan, Singapore and Taiwan value and market share had surprisingly fallen down below than China value in 2003 year. Thus, it seemed that China will be a potential country to compete US hardware production industry after 2003 year.

Reed Electronic Research, Year book Of World Electronic Data (2003) also showed that these computer companies of China had these % of market share : Beijing Founder had 9.9%, Tsinghua Tongtang had 7.8%, dell had 7.2 % , IBM had 5.1% , HP had 4.8% of market share. Thus, it also seemed that China some computer companies will have impotant large market share percentage in global pc sale market. In the future, global hardware production and pc sale industry. China and Taiwan both countries will be one pc manufacturing and design and sale partner. The reason is that China and Taiwan had been the number one rank of markers of notebook pcs, motherboards, scanners, keyboards, add-on card optical drives, monitors and some network equipment etc. pc (personal computer) relative computer function products. It seems that these both countries had co-operated to research any computer relative products to sell to global computer market. They are also the original design manufacturers (DDMS) develop and manufacture over half the world's notebook pcs as well as their customers include all major branded pc vendors (OEMS).

Taiwan Minstry Of Economic Affairs (2003) indicated Taiwan's top notebook ODMS include: In 2003 year volume (thousands) Quanta had $8,500 sale volume thousands , for example, Quanta major OEM partners include Gateway, Dell, HP, IBM, Apple , Sharp, Sony, Fujitsu-Siemens (F/S). Compal had $6,000 sale volume (thousands) , Compal major OEM partners include Dell, HP, F/S, Toshiba, Acer. Thus, it also implied Taiwan had many small size and non famous brand of computer companies which choose to co-operate to be partners with some global large size and famous brand of computer companies to raise competitive effort in global computer market, such as Dell, IBM, HP, Gatway, Apple etc.

Thus, the future trend of computer new product manufacturing development will shift from US to Taiwan and SE Asia, then to China. However, what kind of knowledge work factors will be needed to China and Taiwan . In general, notebook manufacturing stages will include: The first process is design stage, it includes concept design, such as analyze need, create concept and set brand image as well as product planning, such as business case, specifications, industrial design and sourcing strategy. The second process is development stage, it includes design review steps, such as design review, such as mock-ups, electrical test as well as prototype build, such as commercial samples, integrated system test as well as pilot production, such as production process design, pilot. Final process is production stage, it includes mass production, such as ramp-up, volume production, production testing and global distribution as well as sustaining support, such as speed bump, component replacement, technical support and warranty support. Thus, I believe that China and Taiwan must own thee knowledge work skillful of computer design and development professionals who can assist these two countries how to innovate their future computer development to change global traditional computer model to be renew and innovate computer model in the future.

Due to computer industry's stages of development and manufacturing are closely linked , need manufacturability , testing of sample products, concept design and product planning stay together in lead markets and branded vendors, design and development can be separated organizationally and geographically. Thus, China and Taiwan choose to co-operate to exchange their different skill, such as either China has own more concept design and product planning skill or more development skill or more production skill. Then, China will choose either one of the most beneficial comparative advantage among of them. To bring this one of the most beneficial co-operative advantage to attract Taiwan to choose either one of the beneficial comparative advantage of skill, such as either design or development or producton to already co-operate to compete the Western developed country US together.

Thus, US won't be the global computer industry development leader if both US country famous and large employee number computer companies, such as IBM and

Apple which choose to outsource their pc design and development and production skill to China and Taiwan both countries to help them to develop global computer design and development and production skill to be upgraded. Thus, I feel these both countries will plan how to co-operate to compete US to win the global computer industry leader position in the future.

When China invented its (AI) learning system success. Why does it influence global computer industry market change? For example, in the future, instead of global computer manufacters need to consider the design, development and production processes, who also need to consider what factors can influence consumers' laptop purchases. Because any consumers have much different computer model and brand to choose to make final decision to buy any computers. If the computer manufacturer can predict what factors will be whose weakness(es) to influence global computer consumers to change whose mind or attitude to choose to buy other brands of computers, then it won't lose its many old computer customer numbers and reduces it market share in global computer market share.

Nowadays, in general computer has three kinds to provide to global consumers to choose to buy , such as laptop, notebook computers, desktops. it seems that laptop and notebook computers and desktops will have different factors to influence any consumers to choose to buy any brand of computer products. Thus, computer indsutry can divide three consumer groups, such as (stayers, satisfied switchers and dissatisfied switchers) of a computer company with respect to the factors influencing consumers' laptops or notebook computers or desktops purchases. However, I feel the factors can include such as core technicl features, post purchase services, prices and payment conditions, peripheral specification, physical appearance, value added features and connectivity and mobility seven main factors that are influencing consumers' laptop or notebook computer or desktop purchases in global computer industry market.

Ganesh et al., (2000) indicates the customer base of a company consists of three groups of consumers: stayers, satisfied switchers and dissatisfied switchers. Therefore, the consumers in this study replied to the question about whether the current brand that who were using was their first laptop brand or whether who had switched from a previous laptop brand. As a following question, consumers who had switched were asked to state the reason of why who switched from a previous laptop brand brand to their current brand. The options include overall dissatisfaction from the previous laptop brand and reasons other than dissatisfaction. Thus, computer companies need to know what factors influence either whose prior computer customers why who don't choose repeat to buy its any computer products or whose new potential computer customers why who don't choose to buy its any computer products in the first time choice. Thus, future computer manufacturers need to consider intangible salespeople service attitude or performance, such as salespeople current purchase and post purchase service, e.g. technical repair, model function explanation how to use the computer, instead of tangible product performance, e.g. computer appearance design , function , mobility and internet and document download speed connectivity function. Because salespeople and technicians' service performance can be represented to the computer image. If they can provide excellent service to let computer buyers to feel satisfactory, then they can help their computer company employer to build good image. So, staff service performance will be one important factor to influence computer consumers to make the final decision to choose to buy the brand of computer products more easily. Even, one famous brand computer company, such as IBM, Apple, Gateway, these any one of famous brand computer company must not attract any new (the first time) or repeat computer buyers to choose to buy their any kind of computer products , such as laptop, desktop or notebook more easily due to their famous brand. Althoug, these famous computer companies had built good image to let consumers have more confidence to buy any kind of their computer products. But, if these famous computer companies‘ salepeople or repair technicians can not provide excellent customer service or performance to satisfy their computer buyers’ service need, e.g. explaining how to use the new computer, repair post purchase service etc. I believe these famous brands of computer consumers will not have more desire to prefer to chose to buy any one of these famous computer brand’s products. Otherwise, if the other less famous computer companies‘ any kind of laptop, desktop or notebook sale price is higher than the famous brand of computer companies’ products sale price, but their salepeople or technicians can provide more excellent service attitude or performance to satisfy their consumers‘ needs. It is possible that the new or first time computer buyers or repeat computer buyers will still choose to buy their computers. So, the famous or less famous computer brand is not one important factor to influence the computer buyer to decide either to buy the computer or not buy the computer. Otherwise, computer company’s salepeople and repair technician whose service performance or attitude will be one important intangible factors to influence any first time (new) or repeat computer consumers to choose to buy any famous or less famous brand of computer company's product, instead of the tangible computer design appearance and reliable function and convenient mobility and long term durability etc. factors influences.

Thus, China has possible to influence global office and home computer comsumers to choose to buy its any brands of computers to use if it can invent (AI) learning systems to assist global computers to raise their performance efficiency. So, it will influence global computer consumers to choose its country's any brands of computers to buy to use, due to themselves new (AI) learning computers can help office and home computer users to raise efficiency and provide the excellent productive performance to them more than the traditional computers.

1 Can culture factor influence the (AI) computer consumer choice?

When China's (AI) computer learning system has developed in success. Then, it will possible to influence global consumers' traditional computer applying culture to change to new innovation (AI) learning computer applying culture. It means that China will dominate global computer consumer choice to be trended to choose to buy China's any computer brands' produducts , due to it 's (AI) technology can be invented to apply to traditional computers in order to raise their efficiency and reduce office staffs' workload and provide excellent performance to serve office or home (AI) learning computer users.

Durmza and Zengin, (2011:53) indicted marketers closely interested in this issue to know the family which changed and renewed in course in time. It provides an advantage for a marketer to know the family structure and its consumption characteristics. Nowadays, consumer behavior is influenced not only by consumer personalities and motivation, but also by the relationships within families. Family is a social group and it can be considered a crucial place in th perception of marketing (Durmaz, Yakup, CELLK, Mucahit and ORUC, Reyhan, (2011).

The consumer buying behaviors examined through an empirical study. Then, it brings this question: Whether cultural factors will influnece the computer consumer choice. Choice and include computer brand choice, computer price choice, computer model choice, computer design choice, laptop or desktop or notebook product choice, new or second-hand old computer choice, the computer of manufacturing country choice, computer package choice etc. So, any consumer will consider to choose any one of these to decide to buy which kind of computer.

Every country computer consumers had different culture to influence their computer shopping choice. I feel culture can be explained how to influence to computer shopping such as: How do the country computer consumers buy and use their computer products habitually ? How do the country computer consumers react to th computer price changes, attractive advertising methods to satisfy whose needs and computer company store interiors? What underlying mechanisms operate to produce any one of the country computer consumers' responses? If computer marketers have answers to such these questions, who can make better managerial decisions how to adopt which computer target country (countries) consumers' culture.

Consumer behavior deals with many other issues, for instance (Priest, Carter and Statt, 2013: 19). How do we get information about products? How do we assess alternative products? How do different people choose or use different products? How do we decide on value for money ? How much risk do we take with what products? Who influences our buying decisions and our use of the product? How are brand loyalties formed and changed? For computer industry, it means that how computer consumers get information about computer products, how computer consumers assess alternative notebook, desktop, laptop computer products, how different age, country, culture, sex, student or working people or retired people computer consumers choose or use different kind of computer products, such as notebook, desktop, laptop computer products, how much risk computer consumers take with notebook, desktop, laptop computer products, the computer consumers' buying decisons and their use of the desktop or notebook or laptop computer products will be influenced by whom, e.g. family, friends, teacher, employer, computer salepeople, advertisement marketer etc. , computer company brands how are formed and changed by whom, e.g. computer consumers, computer company competitors, marketers, different countries' culture etc.

Durmaz and Jablonski, (2012:56) also explained culture is the essential character of a society that distinguishes it from other cultural groups. The underlying elements of every culture are the values, language, myths, customs, laws and the artifacts or products that are transmitted from one generation to the next (Lamb, Hair and Deniel, 2011: 371). Culture is the most fundamental determinant of a person's wants and behavior. Whereas, lower creatives are governed by instinct, human behavior is largely learned. The child growing up in a society leans a basic set of values, perceptions, preferences and behaviors through a process of socialization involving the family and other social roles.

So, I feel different country have different culture to influence as well as different country computer consumers who have different computer purchase and consume habitually. So, computer manufacturers ought focus on manufacturing the unique need and characteristics to satisfy any country's consumers' needs.

What is my idea about future global computer competition and factors influence computer consumer behavior ?

In conclusion, future computer industry development will trend that computer manufacturers need to consider every country's computer comsumer culture. Because every country computer consumers who will have different computer consumption habitually if who can predict what the country most computer consumers culture, then they can have more confidence to sell their computers to different country markets. Moreover, US computer manufacturers need to consider China and Taiwan computer manufacturing technology because it is possible that these both countries will be its main competitor among different computer manufacuring countries. Because thess both countries will cooperate to research new model of different computers to attract global computer consumers to choose to buy their new model of computer products in the future. Finally, computer manufacturers need to consider salepspeople and repair technicians service performance because computer consumers will consider intangible service performance , instead of tangible computer quality and price and style etc. factors . The main reason is that any computer have chance to be needed to repair and salespeople' skill will influence the computer consumer to make final decision to choose to buy the brand of computer. Thus, these factors will influence global computer development and trend in the future.

Artificial Intelligent Robot: Technology change traditional production of factor model

1 What is mean of (AI) Technological innovation production of factor ?

Can (AI) robot technological learning system change future traditional production of factors model: land, human, equipment and capital to any organizations in order to replace these production of factors and assist organizational development efficiently and effectively?System may be physical , like the solar system or an ecological system or which may be simply behavioral, like an organization. For example, a national economy may be a system, markets are systems, firms and factories are systems. Even, families and individuals are economic systems. The economy of the largest systems, national economy, may be called macroeconomy, which deals in terms of national aggregates for output, income, productivity. The economics of small systems, which are their parts or subsystems may be called microeconomics.

This is traditional production of factor model. for example, a system transforms inputs into outputs. An economic system is such a process. For example, factories are as systems take in raw materials, services etc. and change them into products for sale, i.e. output and consume them, thereby transforming them into rubbish, incidential is bad output. Also, countries consume their actural resources to enhance their standard of living and change them into waste products. If the system in question is national economy, some of the subsystems are might consider to be: the government, the firms, the consumers, the natural resources which it has at its disposal. Each subsystem is itself composed of subsystem of a lower order, such as a firm and each of these can be decomposed into further subsystems, depending on the purpose of the analysis. " All subsystems" interact need have individual characteistics, i.e. they are synergistic if they expected to raise producivity or efficiency or effectively. So, it needs high technological assistance to raise whose ability in economic view.

However, an economic system must continually adapt and restructure to meet the challenges of a changing economic environment if it is to prosper. For example, a firm must respond to its environment in the form of it customers' needs threats from its competitors, government regulations etc. Nowadays, technological innovation process and the nature of social economic and social changes which is occurring as the same time. So, organizations need to have strategic management to raise technological innovation to achieve raising productivity and efficiency aim. In the futue, (AI) robots will be possible one kind of new production of factor to assist organizational development and raise manufacturing efficiency and staffs' working performance in every team.

2 How does (AI) technological innovation occur in economic process?

What is economic process? It consists of the production and consumption of products and services by human. It is a process devised by human for own benefit pupose only. In the past, human lack advanced technological invention, e.g. family society required a much greater degree of organizational skill than hunting and gathering, it seems farming society does not need to achieve efficiency or productivity aim, because it is not industralized manufacturing society. Nowadays, the investment of resourcs is required for manufacturing processes for factories. The manufacturing stage thus needs machines, but it extends the economic process into the processing of manufacturing things, such as food. So, the knowledge and skills to do this are much more specialized again than farmer's or hunter's. So, technological innovation is needed to raise efficient productivity in factories, e.g. the increasing skills of manufacturing and the use of more intensive energy resources, such as coal and oil, gas, even solar energy either resources are from the sun or resources are from earth, e.g. fuels , heat, light, sound utilitiesm liquids , gases,solids. So, technological innovation is important to influence our economic development in our societies.

Economists usually classify what who call future of production into land, labor and capital. Why technological innovation is one another factor of production. For example, the economic process indicates that the first step is resources from the earth, e.g. solar energy supplies to earth to satisfy human needs. In the economic process, it needs these both supplies, driving force of transformation energy supply and captalyst , such as skills, knowledge, organization, creativity, creative participation in consumptions supply. Then, manufacturers shall change these both supplies to production and distribution of ordered materials and utilities in the economic process. Finally, it will provide to human consumption and human spent resources returned to earth in the final step. Another example of the elements of the economic process: the input is driving force of transformation stage of energy sources, e.g. sunlight firewood, oil and gas, coal , nuclear and household and industrial waste. Next is the economic process stage: facilitators, it includes tangible facilitator includes skills, knowledge, organization, creativity, e.g. language, science, technology, industry, machine, politics, law and order, defence, strategic plan, information systems, administration, tangible facilitator includes incentive system, e.g. money, banking, insurance, shares, private or public organizations, markets, land area. Finally, is the product of innovation stage, it includes utilities , such as electricity , heat, light, sound, motive power as well as ordered materials (products) , such as bread, meat, mine, shoes, clothes, houses, television, roads (public goods) etc. In future, (AI) robotic development will be possible participate to new economic process in order to raise global efficiency and performance for every businesses.

3 How (AI) robotic innovation information factor influences the product successful sale

What is the role of (AI) robotic innovation information (big data gathering method) ? Any markets requires product or service suppliers rationally act on the basic such information. But what who can't know in advance is how all the other participants are going to behave. The market clearing price would already be known. There would in fact be agreed prices and which everything could be exchanged, and there would be no market system at all. And so who come to market to settle the price/quantity relationship. The theory is that which will arrive at a single price and quantity which reflect supply and demand. However, the number of interactions or pieces of information to be transmitted doubles with every new participants. However, the requirement for information is not limited to the particular market in question. A compromise between the number of people needed to make more nearly " perfect" in the economic sense, and the quantity of information needed to allow it to arrive at a unique price/quantity relationship. The concept of degrees of freedom is widely used in different technological forms, e.g. engineering industry, the equipment is used by manufacturers to make pencils will be worn out to some extent in the process, and this forms an energy path straight to earth from the market in which the equipment was bought. Similarly wear and tear on the equipment used to make the intermediates and the raw materials will also form direct paths to earth from the markets in which were bought. It seems technological innovation factor of production can bring the pencil stationery product innovation when the new pencil stationey product is produced the more excellent quality by the new machines innovation.

In an economic system which is working " perfectly" according to the definitations, output is therefore a function of available energy and the technological skills to apply it to conversion of inputs into materials and utilities . In a market economy, given the availability of inputs of energy and materials, and the necessary information, the only factor which can bring this about in the long term is a change in the energy efficiency of its conversion process, i.e. the energy consumed unit of output of the same total production. This depends in the application of skills and design, that is technology factor of production.

Why (AI) big data gathering information can influence product sale ability. For example, the commodity is technologically complex like a computer, an aircraft or even a refrigetator. One is buying not just the piece of equipment, but also its specification because few people would understand the parts of the machine, let alone be able to judge their quality. Furthermore, one is also buying the future performance of the machine in operationm , its fuel consumptionm reliability, service costs, length of life, resistance to obsolescence etc. Probably the only guarantee that any information obtained on these points is valid is the reputation of the manufacturer. Purchasers estimate chose chances of surviving the guarante period. Brand names are a way of simplisfying information flows. Such problems of defining the commodity and so handling the information necessary to arrive at a stable price, are magnified when counterfeit products, such as are flooding on to the market at present, find their way into markets for genuine products. Buyers will be unable to distinguish unless who are experts and sometimes that may need chemical analysis or destructive testing. This is a recent phenomenon to buy technological products.

4 Why does (AI) big data gathering information technology influence the real market system change ?

Can (AI) big data gathering information technology be one kind of production of factor to influence the real market system change to be more fast speed of market information communication in global industries? The market system in the real world includes: the first is manual work (manpower) element, in effect the provision of an elementary utility for consumption in a conversion process. If labors are not providing manpower, who become unemployed. Unemployment is not simply leaving a resource at a particular time, it is an injustice and a burden one the very real society which economics is supposed to help. Moreover, the unemployed can't spend the money who don't earn, and so buyers are reward from the economic process. The second is catalytic skills, knowledge, organization and creativity element which applied to the conversion processes which turn raw materials into products and utilities for consumption. In this case, who are as varied as the individuals that make up mankind, their accumulated knowledge, their capability of organising themselves to achieve their ends and not least their creativity,the ability to generate entirely new catalytic effects. Finally, is the incentive element, which is the prospect of participating in comsumption of the products of the economic process. The incentive system is cash for current or future exchange for products and utilities. The incentive system must be within the control of the social system of which it is a part. It can only be addressed by society as the whole system. However, for the individual and the firm too the creative must by definition come from outside and it is also depend on the rest of society.

What kinds of product can link between markets to increase speed of market information communication when global industries choose to apply (AI) big data gathering information technology to gather global competitors‘ product and client and price etc. business data. However, there are products which are linked in a different way by associated use. For products anyone who buys a vehicle must also be prepared to buy its fuel, tyres etc. A decision to buy the vehicle therefore automatically generates subsequent expenditure in the other markets. These markets are not so much competitors for buyers' money as complementary to each other. Sale in one must lead to sales in the other. This technological products have the same point, it is that which are needed to attempt to innovate their quality to raise their competitive ability to win their competitors. It seems that (AI) big data gathering information technological innovation can be a factor production to these different brands of vehicles and which related link products. Much the same occurs in technological industry. A company may feel that it is wise to buy related pieces of equipment from the same manufacturer, especially if they have to be connected in some way, whatever the price, within reason.

5 Can (AI) big data gathering timing of information influence real marketing system?

The analysis has shown that two sorts of (AI)big data gathering information are essential of the market is to reach " equilibrium" values of price and quantity: information concerns on the economic environment, which participants can obtain before the market opens; and information about the process of bargaining displayed, which can only be made available as the bargaining proceeds. However, buyers and sellers happen next. If the information acts as a reference point, it can only be a historical one. This is particularly so where markets operate continuously. There is always a lapse between the conclusion of deals and their display, so that new deals are always influenced to be not update information , in the absence of the most recent data, if dealing is busy. So, timing of information ought to be kept the most update to let buyers can have more confidence to make final choice to buy the broad of products. The quality of information which had to passed during bargaining in order to achieve on a unique price/quantity relationship increased rapidly with the number of participants because of the need of to allow everyone of buyers to interact with all the others.

It follows therefore, that as the number of participants becomes very large, the necessary information flows become much larger still and the time needed to allow this to take place increases greatly. So, timing of information can influence the participants would have changed or would have not changed their minds or gone home before proceedings could draw to a close. So, price and quality is the main message of information to influence consume individual attitude to decide to buy the product in market.

Timing of information can influence business cycles. It is well known that business activity is cyclinal. The short cycles of 4 to 5 years are best established , but consumers believe who can discern longer term and even very long term cycles of activity with periods of up to 50 years. Cyclical behavior, can only occur where these is an imperfect response to change, because of imperfect information. In general, this sort could not caused by the response time behavior of individual markets. Whatever the nature of the link, it is clearly the case that the price/quality relationship in individual markets is varying independently of the factors which might normally be expected to affect it in isolated systems. So, cyclical phenomena in business are strong evidence of the market process network behaving as a system.

In conclusion, markets are activites to exchange products and services. The elements of economic chains together to allow modern industrial economies or (AI) big data gathering information technological economy to function with all their complexity. They are essential to change and they permit innovation. However, markets are not well represented by the conventional supply/demand schedules, in particular because these can not include the effects of time as an variable factor. It is much clear to represent timing of information as systems in the form of flow diagrams showing the movement of products from innovative processes through markets to consume. Revenue from the market then supplies feedback to product manufacturers, and the whole system responds at different rates to different levels of feedback from clients. An effective medium of exchange is necessary for proper responses to be made. The complexity of the modern world, where price and quantity and quality in the market are all can't exist without the timing of information factor influence. Price signals are often confused by products, imperfect or incomprehensible information and the various effects of time, and in any case quantities to be supplied to the market have to be decided well in advance of market day. The whole trend a modern industrial economy or technological economy is towards product differentiation. Such as mobile phone, laptop computer etc. technologic products. Manufacturers often need to innovate design, quality, functions to adapt to client's individual need. So, technological innovation is often a production of factors to invent high technological products. Services too can't be fitted into price/quantity schedules because it is impossible to define the product. Otherwise, the categorisation of human as labor, having a price/ quantity relationship, when who are clearly , each is an individual learning system, changing every day of whose life and changing the economic process accordingly. In fact, human must necessarily be accepted as a feature of modern life, to protect to let them to enjoy high quality of life. So, individual economic stage will be needed to enter technological economic stage in economic environment. Indeed by limiting the rate of change such actions may in no small measure be a condition of stability for the people in an economy . It seems that (AI) big data gathering information technological innovation is one factor of production and it has close relstionship to timing of reasonable price and quality information to persuade consumers to choose to buy the manufacturer's product.

6 (AI) big data gathering information can reduce the cost basis of economic activity to any businesses

(AI) big data gathering information technology can help any organizations to reduce the time and human effort economic cost. In conversion processes there is always some wear and tear of the fixed asset, the equipment, building etc. which reduce their capacity to produce in future. Of course after the money has been spent on the plant, it is no longer cost of operating. This is not technological obsolescence which results from development of better ways of meeting market needs. The efficiency of produrers is continually improved and the most effective use of the resources available is continually improved and the most effective use of the resources available to the society, and the most effective use of the resources available to the society is made according to the criteria of economic values. The under-utilised resources locked up in the inefficient operation are not necessarily lost. The producer may learn in time to use them better. So that who can eventually compete on moral equal terms, or who may give way to another who knows how to manage the resources more efficiently. If however, the inefficiency has a deep-rooted cause which can not be remedied, or even a producer who is capable of improvement but refuses to act, then the resources run down to extiaction faster than ordinary wear and tear would cause them to. So, it suppose to technological innovation can help producers to reduce cost for long term. It is cost benefit to producers for long term.

For agricultural industry example, it was said that the only way for a farmer to increase whose not revenue significantly, once who was farming as efficiently as possible, was to increase the area of land under cultivation. But technological innovation is such production of factor, it might be a case for increasing the area under cultivation in order to make better use of a piece of equipment, such as a tractor, and so spread its cost over more production. Another might be in the processing industries, such as petrochemicals or oil where many new producers with the same global threats and opportunities. The input costs when products or utilities move in the direction of time and energy in the economic process. If one opportunity for using the resources is selected, then another potential use will be foregone. Opportunity costs are therefore distinguished from input costs by time. So, the production for factor of technological innovation can be opportunity cost, if the manufacturer felt who can spend less manufacturing expenditure for long term. Due to who lose to use money to spend other expenditure or invest, who choose to invent technological innovation to reduce long term input costs. The best opportunities are those which maximise prices and minimise costs. SO, (AI) big data gathering technology can be applied to agricultural industry to help farmers to reduce farming time and farming equipment cost to grow any fruit, vegetable and rise , tomotato , potato etc. food in production of factor view.

Producers try to achieve higher market prices by giving their products some distinguishing feature which whose hope will attract buyers away from other competitors and /or generate new buyers, what marketers call product differentiation. In effect they try to move their product into a new market, perhaps thought of as " up market" or a " market niche", but certainly in separate market for analytical purpose. Even if they can not do this, which is unusual in these days of increasing technological innovation and communication , operators continually try to improve their processes in order to reduce costs. If always requires the investment of new resources, e.g. technological innovation.

In the real world, it is not possible to differentiate products or processes except in time. The overall result is to move the process in the direction of economic improvements, in effect the behavior of economic system as a learning system. Time introduces all the risks and opportunities which present themselves to the processor. In the analysis which follows , we classify and illustrate the various aspects of economy of scope under the traditional economic heading of labor, capital, and land. Energy and information, technological innovation are considered too ,because which are fundamental to all systems and process in economic activity.

7 The (AI) big data gathering technological innovation benefits

First, (AI) big data gathering technological innovation can bring to help organizations to reduce staff number and divide labor to raise different department work efficiency and performance benefits. For the division of labor benefits example. This is a complex process into stages in which a worker can specialize, thus allowing who to perform that particular task more efficiently, i.e. at lower cost per unit of effective output than if who had to undertake the whole process. Such an improvement in efficiency results from the more effective learning, greater development of skills and more intensive application over a period of time which becomes possible when a task is easily within the capacity of one person.

It is easily confused with advances in (AI) big data gathering technology, capital investment or scale of operation. Division of complex process into stages may subsequently allow the development of specialised technologies for the individual stages, and this may result in specialised equipment, and hence capital investment . Similiarly, if the process is carried out with less labor and/or lower raw material costs for each unit of output, those concerned may in principle decide either the produce more . Output or the produce the same output with less input. It seems technological innovation can bring low cost benefits. In fact, new technology imposes a diseconomy on the old, eg. functions using old technology are at a cost disadvantage and must adopt or eventually disappear under free competition. So, new technology is the source of growth and adoptation in economy. The solutions to a diseconomy of scape lies in a change of scope, for example, in this case different establishments operating at different times, and perhaps with different prices. If capital investment are differentiated be improved to give longer life and better use, which in effect reduces their cost in use. For example, continuing advantages in technology allow processes to be designed in such a way that which deliver the same output with ever decreasing inputs of materials, labor or energy. Thus waste is minimised by planning and the conservation of process energy, and maintenance is reduced by change of design or the use of new materials. It may often worth spending more on equipment initially to reduce those time dependent costs. This sort of efficiency is the most obvious effect of scope rather than scale.

Deterioration and obsolescence means wear and tear are the changes which occur in artefacts as which are used , i.e. deterioration , or changes in quality or scope with time. These are not simply time effects because which depend both on the original design and on the conditions of use, such as maintenance skills and even simple care and attention. Obsolescence is difference to depreciation, it relates to the battle in the market place . The networks of markets brings products and therefore all conversion processes into competition for the same revenues. Old products will be not popular because which become harder to sell. Obsolescence, therefore depends not only on time, but also on competition, in the same time of business. It seems technological innovation can avoid obsolescence occurrence to old products to raise which competitive ability to the same markets. However, there was hardly an element in the competitive cost structures of conversion processes which was not disturbed in a way which differentiated country form country, industry from industry and firm from firm, such as (AI) big data technological innovation to any old products, which production of factor cost structures is the same basically.

8 What is the relationship between the process of (AI) big data gathering technological innovation and the

production of factor?

The term "innovation" is used to describe the deliberate process by which a new product or process comes to be sold in the market. Technology innovation can be applied to conversion processes, which requires the use of energy, or their products, which have an economic energy content. It is therefore a function of all the forces which shape markets: manufacturing, processing, technology, buying, selling, information, prices costs etc. So an innovating organization may be a whole company or it may be an individual. Other forms of innovation (production of factor) relate to the sale of services within what defines as the facilitiation system. That sort of exchange is not specifically considered to be one production of factor, because it involves different adoptation processes and response times, and doesn't of itself add to the quantity of products or utilities sold.

However, invention can not be defined to one production of factor and it is to be distinguished to innovation. We can describe invention is as the process of discovering something completely new, i.e. a new fact or relationship. It is an important scientific advance. Invention enlarges the scope of man's awareness, but it doesn't necessarily have direct economic value in itself. If it is sold, it is the sale of an idea, an exchange of a little creativity for an incentive within the facilities system. It isn't marketed as a new product of a conversion process. No energy of conversion is involved. The great majority of inventions do not enter into the economic process and which do not become innovations until that happens.

If the change of scope results in a new (AI) manufacturing technological process for making a product or utility which is already being sold, this can't be differentiated from the existing product or utility in the market concerned. To be successful the new process must make it at lower unit cost than existing process. The result then is that either the price of the product fulls and processes to improve are imposed to competition or more net revenue is accumulated. So the aims of the factors of technological innovation production include: The introduction of a process for making at a lower unit cost a non-differentiated product which is sold into a commodity market, and the development and sale of a differentiated product which will draw buyers away from other markets, or draw money into the market which would not otherwise have been spent.

The nature of (AI) manufacturing technological innovation how causes factor of production. The process of technological innovation is the arrangement of materials at the elementary, say atomic or molecular level, or of components or the design of new machines, or of the relative positions of components, for example, the location of nodes in networks. There are the three levels at which the scope of the economic process may be changed. However, technological innovation can't seem without some change in the way materials ae ordered. It follows that all technological innovation flows initially from some change in a conversion process. Thus technological in the result of investment in conversion processes, where investment is defined as laying down fixed assets and so it requires a change in the use of energy consumed during conversion to make useful products. The flexible manufacturing system themselves are examples of the third level of innovation, the spatial arrangement of components and hence the link between them. Patterns of communication have changed and are continue to change as a result of new technoloby in the use of energy and the convergence of computer, data maipulation and telecommunication. Flexible manfacturing systems manufacture components in rather than having them made by supplies industries and transported to an assembly plant in batches. The new arrangements reduce both the time of reponse to market changes and all the skills of components which are needed to give flexibility of response in conventional systems , i.e. they give economy of scope.

9 How to response times in (AI) manufacturing technological innovation?

In the terminology which have developed above, the behavioral effects may be considered as adjustment of the scope of the sellers and buyers organizations as the process of acceptance of the innovation in the market proceed. Costs and risks in technological innovation, innovation requires the commitment of resources over a long period, and it is therefore subject to the same kind of risks as any investment in conversion processes. The most obvious risk is that the technological difficulties are in the initial concept, with the result that no returns will be earned and the resources sunk in the investment may have been wasted. There is a set of market-related reasons why technological success may not result in an innovation. By the time, the new process or product is ready for the market, the demand for it may have receded or may never have materialised. This may be the result of fulfiment of the potential users' needs by another technology, i.e. the innovation may be technologically obsolete before it may be because of a change of fashion or styles of living.

Two conclusions may be drawn, firstly, the product manufacturer has a good foresight and understanding is needed when undertaking projects which consume large amount of capital, or it may result in gross waste, because the future is always uncertain, however, the analysis, secondly, there is a limit to the rate of constructive innovation in an economic system, the ratio at which the system can accumulate. Hence, some product manufacturer will feel the technological innovation can be a good production of factor , such as a cost advantage is termed a competitive advantages. It is a broader term than the comparative advantages of traditional economy because of does not depend on a favorable climate or an abundance of natural resource. It is developed and maintained entirely by the skills of the people in the firms which are involved.

Technology is like on the economic process, because once knowledge about transforming inputs into outputs has been obtained, and especially after it has been implemented, it doesn't disappear. Technological innovation moves the whole process. Thus, economy of scope confer permanent advantages on those who have them. Economy of scope is to be obtained from all the elements of the economic process which change with time and these are suspectible to improvement, whether as separate elements. They involve people, and their capacity to learn and improve, and material in all their different forms.

10 Why technological innovation will be one factor of

production to technological manufacture industry.

Innovation is the process by which new products' processes methods or services are created. Innovation offers added value for and users by providing better and/or cheaper functionality than previous options. Innovation combines changes in technology, business models, organization etc. The basic idea may be a new technical solutions, a new business model or a change in organization. In a competitive economy, no business can survive long term without updating its products and services or the ways in which are produced or delivered. Innovation policy must promote renewal across all business sectors and not just focus on high technological industries.

Since most innovations are complex and each subsystem has its own limitation , an important part of the innovation process is finding the right balance between conflicting demands. In most cases, there are several possible ways of providing a new function to users, or possible applications of a new technology. Which combination of features the market will prefer can't be predicted with any certainty. Whether the origin was a market opportunity on a new technological capability to one part of the production of factor to the product.

Innovation integrates knowledge from a number of different fields: technology, marketing, design, economic etc. In the production of factor view, it is hard to collect all the necessary competences in a single organization. Because technological products need to be updatd to keep competition in market. Thus, innovation has become a process of constant with suppliers and competitors, with consultants and with academic researchers. In the production of factor view, the capacity to innovate depends on how well different parts of this system are adapted to each other and how well they work together.

Today, the relationship between science and innovation is more complex and interdependent. Science-based technologies, such as microelectronics or biotechnology could not have been developed without scientific understanding, but modern science is equally dependent on advanced technology. Economists tend to prefer technology performance standards, but these risk favouring marginal improvements to existing technologies when discouraging more radical, long term solution. Also, economists tend to think of innovation as a production processes. A more production describes innovations as an experimental learning proces in which organizations and individuals build new competence. This term "research-based competence" is rather than " science-based knowledge or "scientific information".

I shall argue that economists‘ active process is a better way of think about the relationship between industry and academic research. Whether can the production of factor of technological innovation make use of the tools and results of research in addressing real world problem to manufacture any technological products? This main concern at the time was whether research and innovation were essentially different activities which should be supported in different ways or whether it was important to deal with both aspects together since which were interdependent. However, innovation is a process of searching, experimenting and learning. Consumers can learn about how new products, processes and services are created, how firms build competence for this and what information sources which use. So, I feel technological innovation ought be one part of production process or production of factor to some manufacturers. Such as, searching is needed for better ways of doing worth which things. Experimenting is needed because consumers can't seen in advance the best way of accomplishing a desired outcome or indeed what users really want or need. Learning is needed because actors involved in an innovation process will learn from it. The kind of learning which changes consumers' ability to solve future challenges and opportunities. However, economists often think of innovation is as a production prcocess, where knowledge transformed into a new product. We measure research and development investment, relating these to outcomes in the form of patents, new products and productivity or economic growth. Innovations are not just new technological products or processes, it also mentions organizational innovations, new distribution channels, new business models etc. In fact, it is often misleading to think about technical or organizational innovation as separate processes. Most innovations combine changes in technology, business models organization etc. in production process.

What kinds of product can belong to high technological manufacturing. For example, the world's most advanced steel plants and paper mills can never be classified as high technology because of their complementary need for high levels of investment in fixed capital, and aerospace manufacture is classified as medium technology. The standard definition of high technology measures research and development intensity not the generation or use of advanced technology as such. A far better measure is the proportion of scientists, engineers and highly qualified technicians in the labor force. For computer industry example, innovations in the field of rabotic manufacturing, nanotechnologies and human genetics research all have been enabled by low cost computational and control capabilities supplied by computers and software. Reducing the cost of software important objectives of the U.S. software industry. However, the complexity of the software industry to support the U.S. is computerized economy is increasing at an alarming rate. Software nonperformance and failure are expensive. In actuality many factors contribute to the quality issues facing the software industry. These include marketing strategies, limited liability by software vendors, and decreasing returns to testing.

At the core of these issues is the difficulty in defining and measuring software reliability, usability, efficiency, maintenability and portability. Information problems are further complicated by the fact that even with substantial testing, software developers don't truly know how their products with perform until who encounter real scenarios. The similiar industries with need have technological innovation in the productive process (production of factor), such as automotive and aerospace equipment manufacturers and related electronic communications equipment manufacturers. Quality is defined as attribute factor to different kinds of software product. Defining the attributes of software quality and determining the metrics to access the relative value of each attribute are not formalized processes. Because users place different values on each attribute depending on the product's use, it is important that quality attributes be observable to consumers. The technological innovation is one production of factor to software industry. Due to software attributes have those accurateness, interoperability, security, reliability (maturity, recoverability); usability (understandability, learnability, operability); efficiency (time behavior, resource behavior); maintainability (analyzability, changeability, stability, testability); portability (abaptability, installability, replaceability). It seems that due to software attribute have these characteristics, so it causes technological innovation is one production of factor to software industry.

Nowadays, human needs have been increasing, external factor can influence some industries cause technological innovation is one production of factor need. Together, these tends are going to reshape now human live and work, reorganize our social, economic and political institutions and redistribute power and reward in society. In the longer term, as machine learning and computer power intelligence technological innovation needs from consciousness, as machine learning and computer from consciousness, as improving health technologies allow for biological enhancements and species divergence, and as the final frontier is also needed by space travel, technological and social transformation will increasingly change what is means to be human. However, human have to better understand how our world is changing and by what forces those changes are driven . So, because human have high living quality needs, so it causes many new products have technological innovation to manufacture new product or to raise high quality need to satisfy our daily life. It will cause of factor to some products.

The (AI) manufacturing technological innovation factor can influence the economic of the pork meat production in agricultural industry. For example, the economy of the pork meat production on a farm has been carried out with the help of the method of production functions (factor-product and factor-factor). The influence of the weight of an animal on the daily growth tells us that the growth is increased with the increse of the entry weight to 19kg and with the exit weight of the fattened animal of 100 kg. So, the relationship between the daily growth and the feed costs by a feeding day shows us the tendency of than increase of a daily growth with the increase of the feed costs, e.g. with the increase of labor inputs to 2.6 hours/100 kg of the live weight and the increased profit to 29 monetary units. Labor productivity grows with the increase of the capacity usage to 87% and then it decrease. The economy of agricultural production considerably depends on the development of cattle-breeding as a natural capacity of transforming plant products into high quality cattle products. Cattle-raising production influences the food quality, the development of food production industry, the output of high quality and healthy safe product and the development of agricultural economy. So, it seems technological innovation can be a production of factor to influence farm agricultural industry to assist farmers to apply high, e.g. agricultural technology (skills) produces high quality and tastic of farming met to satisfy consumers‘ diet needs.

Growth of total factor productivity (TFP) can provide society with an opportunity to increase the welfare of people. In particular, in the simplest framework, change in labor productivity factor depends on change (TFP) and capital deepening. How to change TFP? I shall suppose the technological innovation method is a factor to reduce labor cost, but it can raise labor productivity and products or goods of quality to satisfy consumers' needs in competitive market. Economists often define the knowledge economy as production and services based on knowledge-intensive activities tht contribute to an accelerated pace of technical and scientific technology, as well as rapid absolescence. Knowledge is now recognized as the driver of productivity and economic growth, leading to a new focus on the role of information, technology and learning in economic performance. In the knowledge-based economy, innovation is driven by the interaction of producers and users in the exchange of both codified and tacit knowledge: This interactive model has replaced the traditional linear model of innovation. The knowledge-intensive and high technology, economy tends to be the most dynamic in terms of output and employment growth. Changes in technology and particularly the advent of information technologies are making educated and skilled labor more valuable, and unskilled labor less. So, the technological innovation production of factor will bring skilled labor needs, more and unskilled labor needs less.

Although, it can maximize the benefits of technology for productivity, but it can raise unemployment number of non-skillful labor, because the high technological product firms will choose to dismiss the non-skillful labor and will employ skillful labor when innovation which decide to apply technological innovation method to produce whose products. For example, output and employment are expanding fastest in high technology industries, such as computers, electronic and aerospace. Also, knowledge-intensive service sectors, such as online education, communication and information(long distance call) are growing even faster, such as internet shopping technological business can be production of factor to let universities can teach students from internet, such as distance learning. Internet can be used to adventise and sell products from businessman individual website more easily. Also, mobile can use internet to do same benefits, such as laptop or desktop kinds of high technological computer products. It seems technological benefits can attract consumer individual consumption more easily. So, skillful biased technical change is a shift in the production technology that favors skilled over unskilled labor by increasing its relative productivity and therefore, its relative demand. In fact, skill-biased technical change is a shift in the production technology (factor of production that favors skilled, e.g. more relative productivity) and therefore, its relative demand.

11 How can external and internal factors affect the product and (AI) manufacturing process innovation?

In fact, the competition advantages of a company strongly depends on its possibility to benefit from innovational activities. Understanding the factors how which affect product and process innovation and their effort is necessary to be proved why innovational activities can be the one part production of factors to some new products. It has close relationship between product and business processes innovation and industry maturity and customer needs (demand) technological opportunities and investment attractiveness and company size and export orientation. These external and internal factors can influence innovational activities to some new products.

Nowadays, fast technology development, combined with

the globalization and fast changes in with the globalization and fast changes in customer demand, implies that a competitive advantage of a company. So, companies will spans great effort in beating the competition innovations have a vital influence on economic development of a country. On the macro level, innovations have a vital influence on economic development that innovations are more and more present both a developed and developing countries that wish to grow developing countries that wish to grow fast and become developed. If we simply categorize companies all innovative or non-innovative. Among different innovation's categorizations is developed by researchers, the most important are: classification according to the type of innovation to degree of innovativity, innovations can be classified as incremental, semi-radical and radical innovations (Davila et al 2006), who indicates that radical innovations potentially offer huge profits and competitive advantage, but demand considerably high risk level, much company effort need and resource engagement. Otherwise, incremental innovations have more modest returns, but demand lower risk level, level of efforts and resources and are generally more successful. Finally, semi-radical innovations are somewhere between the two of them.

According to (Christensen 2003) explained to an innovations can be sustaining and disruptive. Sustaining innovations can be placed in the whole range from incremental to radical and discuptive are either semi-radical or radical. Sustaining innovations are those that improve existing products or process, disregarding the degree of improvement. Disruptive innovations create a huge growth offering a new of performances which has even it is inferior from the start comparing to existing technologies' performances a potential to become superior. Companies are advised to accept what is the best for their situation and design innovational processes, develop aptitudes, allocate resources and form partnerships in compliance to that decision.

In fact, many external and internal factors can affect companies chose product innovations, because process, innovations or their combination, e.g. factors include industry maturity, customer needs and expectations , technological opportunities, investment attractiveness, intensity of cmpetition, company size, origin of ownership and export orientation. In the industry maturity stage, as a market matures and customer needs become defined in a better way, companies transfer the focus of their competition to expenses and economy of range investing more in business processes in order to make them more effective and more efficient. Customer needs and expectations are essential for process innovations that improve process effectiveness. Orientation to customers and their satisfaction are well-known concept in the field of a total quality management.

The point of view that market demand presents the main determine the rate and activities of an invention because each rational company that tends to make profit is responsive to economic stimuli . According to Schmookler (1962) demand growth is prior to the growth in innovative activites, i.e. market requests guarantee stimuli for companies to innovate and take up new technologies. This concept is popularly called " market pull" in a sense that a market pulls innovations.

12 What is (AI) production of factor knowledge economy ?

I shall give evidences to explain why technological innovation can be one kind of production factor to some technological product manufacture industry nowadays. Nowadays, we are entering the knowledge based economy stage. Knowledge is now recognized as the driver of productivity and economic growth, leading to new focus or the role of information technology and learning in economic performance. The knowledge based economy and its relationship is as traditional economics, as reflected in " new growth theory". Because every technological product manufacturer needs workers to acquire a range of skills and to continuously adapt these skills underlines the " learning economy". The importance of knowledge and technology diffusion requires better understanding of knowledge networks and " national innovation systems".

Firstly, knowledge-based economies which are directly based on the production, distribution and use of knowledge and information. The is reflected in the trend in growth in high technology investment, high technological industries, move highly-skilled labor and associated productivity gains. Also required is tacit knowledge including the skills to use and adapt codified knowledge-based economy, innovation is driven by the interaction of producers and users in the exchange of both codified and tacit knowledge.

Employment in the knowledge-based economy is characterized by increasing demand for more highly skilled workers. The knowledge-intensive and high-technology tend to be the most dynamic in terms of output and employment growth. The science system, essentially public research laboratories and institutes of highest education, carries out key functions in the knowledge-based economy, including knowledge production, innovative technology. So, the traditional functions of producing new knowledge through basic research and educating new generations of scientists and engineers with its newer role of collaborating with industry in the transfer of knowledge and technology. For example, our societies tend to research institutes and academic increasingly have industrial partners for financial as well as innovative purposes, but most combines this with their essential role in more generic research and education.

In general, our understanding of what is happening in the knowledge-based economy is constrained by the extent and quality of the available knowledge-rated indicators. So, available knowledge-rated indicated. So, development of indicators of the knowledge-based economy must start with improvements to more traditional input indicators of research and development expenditures and research personal. Better in indicators are also needed of knowledge stocks and flows, particularly relating to the diffusion of information technologies, in both manufacturing and service sectors; social and privates rates of return to knowledge investments to the impact of innovation technology in productivity and growth.

However, knowledge is such as human being (human capital) and in innovative technology has always been central to economic development. When human is entering the 21 ST century, our output and employment are expanding tastes in high technology industries, such as computers, electronics and aerospace investment is thus being directed to high-technology products and services, particularly information and communicating technologies. Computers and related equipment are the fastest growing component of tangible investment. Equally important are more intangible investments in research and development, the training of the labor force, computer software and technical expertise. Hence, it causes employment is growing in high technology, science-based sectors ranging from computers to pharmaceuticals. Also, research and development causes manufacturing sector is losing jobs. Due to those jobs are more highly skilled and pay higher wages than those in lower technology sectors (e.g. textiles and food processing). Knowledge-based jobs in service sectors are also growing strongly. Indeed, non-production or knowledge workers those who don't engage in the output of physical products, are the employees in most demand in a wide range of activities from computer technicians, through physical therapists to marketing specialists.

Economists continue to search for the foundations of economic growth. Traditional, " production functions" focus on labor, capital , materials and energy, land; however, knowledge and technology are external influence on production. Analytical approaches are being developed. So, that knowledge can be included more directly in production functions. Investment in knowledge can raise productive capacity of the other factors of production as well as transform them into new products and processes from innovative technology.

According to the neo-classical production function, returns diminish is as more capital is added to the economy an effect which may be offset, however, by the flow of new technology. In new growth theory, knowledge can raise the returns on investment, which can contribution to the accumulation of knowledge. Technological change can also raise the relative marginal productivity of capital through education and training of the labor force, investment in research and development and the creation of new managerial structures and worth organization. In fact, incorporating knowledge into standard economic production functions is not easy task, as this factor defies some fundamental economic principles, such as that of scarcity, knowledge is intangible, but labor, capital, land, equipment etc. production of factors which can be tangible or measured. However, some kinds of knowledge can be easily reproduced and distributed at lower cost to abroad set of users, which tends to undermine private ownership. Knowledge is a much broader concept than information, which is generally the " know-what", and "know-why" components of knowledge. There are also the types of knowledge which come closet to being market commodities or economic resources to be fitted into economic production functions.

Knowledge can divide know-why and know-how both kinds of concept. Know-why means to scientific knowledge of the principles and laws of nature. This kind of knowledge underlines technological development and product and process advances in most industries. The production and reproduction of know-why is often organized in specialized organizations, such as research-laboratories and universities. Otherwise, know-how means to skills or the capability to do something. Business judging market prospects for a new product or a personnel manager selecting and training staff have to use their know-how. The same is true for the skilled worker operating complicated machine tools. Finally, knowledge-who becomes increasingly important. Know-who involves information about who knows what and who know how to do what. It involves the make if possible to get access to experts and use their knowledge efficiently. So, knowledge economy brings those conditions to our societies. One hypothesis is that globalization and international competition have led to decrease relative demand for less-skilled workers of the phenomenon; an alterative explanation is that innovative technology change has become more strongly biased in favor of skilled workers, changes in firm behavior is as the main reason for falling real wages for low-skilled workers. Thus, innovative technology and knowledge economy has close relationship to cause knowledge workers can bring high technological products of production of factor in technological product manufacture industry.

13 (AI) Production of factor internal technical skill

Secondly, it is the internal skill biased technical change influences. Skill-biased technical change is a shift in the production technology, that flavors skilled over unskilled labor by increasing its relative productivity and , therefore, its relative demand of innovative technology of production factor. The direction of technical changes i.e. whether new capital complements skilled or unskilled labor may be determined by innovators' economic incentives shaped by relative prices, the size of the market and institutions.

Economic theory views the production technology as a function describing that a collection of factor inputs can be transformed into output, and it defines technical change as a shift in the production of function. In fact, given who observed movements of the production function only concentrates on , such as land supply, labor numbers, equipment supply, capital demand factors. Therefore,To make sense of these recent developments, the concept of factor biased technical change can be another production of factor to influence the new technical products quantities change. For example, the timing of the rise in the skill premium has changed the rapid diffusion of information and communication technologies in the workplace environment in any high technological industry generally nowadays. For example, expenditures in information processing equipment and software, is as a share of U.S. private non-residential fixed investment, rose from 6% in 1960 year to 40% in 2000 year. At the heart of those dynamic change.

This is an improvement in the quality and productivity of all those equipment products, relying heavily on semiconductors like computers, software and switching equipment underlying much of communication technology. In the early adoption phase of a new technology, that those who adapt more quickly can reap some benefits. As time goes by, there will be enough makers learning how to work with the new technology to offset the wage differential. Note the difference with the hypothesis set, where the effect of capital deepening on the skill premium is permanent. Also, information technologies production of factor can reduce costs of data storage, communication, monitoring and supervision activities within the firm which causes a shift towards a new organizational design. In particular, the layers in the hierarchical structure can be reduced, so that the organization of the firm becomes "flatter". So, workers no longer perform routinized, responsible for a wide range of tasks within teams. Therefore, adaptable workers verses at multi-tasking activities benefits is a factor of production to reduce internal cost of any firms.

Due to technological innovation causes the layers in the hierarchical structure can be reduced, so that the organization of the firm becomes "flatter". How technological innovation can influence internal skill biased technical change to orgnizational structure. Development behavioral means it is through managment theory. So, high technological skillful organization will choose to apply theory x more than theory y because this technological innovation will reduce some unskillful staffs and give more effort and duties to those skillful staffs to use high technological skill to do whose jobs daily and who will feel lazy and unhappy to do extra more technological jobs. Theory x assumptions are the average human being dislike of work and work avoid if who can, most people must be controlled, directed or threatened with punishment to adequate effort to action organization objective; otherwise, theory y assumptions are people like to use physical and mental effort to work as natural as play and rest, human being dislike work, a source of satisfaction, threat of punishment are not being effort. Hence, technological innovation can cause organizations to change whose structure and skill staffs need to do more jobs. It causes employer need to give extristic and intrinsic motivations to satisfy whose skillful staffs needs to raise efficiency, e.g. giving more tangible reward, as salary, benefit, security, promotion, good contract of condition of work service, comfortable workplace environment as well as using one ability to achieve who feel apprecation, positive being treating of psychological satisfactory needs.

In technological innovation of organization structure, the management committee needs to concern whose skillful technological labor individual psychological needs. Because technological innovation is one important production of factor and it has close relationship between motivation and staff individual efficiency and productivity. As Maslow's hierarchy of needs indicates people (staffs) mean having satisfied to achieve motivation behavior, the lowest love is basic physiological, the need for food, as salary, safe working condition, then is job security, benefit. Next is friendship at work group, after is promotion, payment increasing, high status of job title. Finally is achievement in work advancement opportunitie creative task in related aspect at work motivation. Hence, after the traditional non-technological innoviation of organization changed the technological innovation of organizational structure, management needs to concern that motivation is needed to develop of behavioral through contributed to management theory. Every organiztion manageer needs to know what its team staffs whose indvidual needs, it includes extrinsic needs, e.g. salary, promotion, security as well as intrinsic needs, e.g. achievement, appreciaton. If the employees feel extrinsic needs are more than intrinsic needs, the managers can consider what extrinsic needs, the managers can consider what extrinsic needs of whose employee individual need. If the employee feels intrinsic needs are more than extrinsic needs, the manage can consider what intrinsic needs the employee individual actual need in order to motivate the skillful worker to work efficiently and raising productivity.

After changing the technological innovation of organizational structure, the management needs to concern how to plan to raise its productivity from its production of factor of technological innovation. Planning is looking ahead, control is looking back, every organization must need strategic plan, operative plan and tastic plan for every department to give aim for its mission objectives. Then it needs to achieve its any short term plans or long term plans efficiently, e.g. how to achieve to produce and to sell 5,000 computers sale objective or how to increase to achieve 20% profit or productivity objective from 10% within one year. So, after the technological innovation production of factor influences the organization needs to find reasons what how to influence it can not achieve these new objectives within one year. Then, it needs to find reasons and revises to solve challenges to control it can achieve it's planning objectives. For example, SWOT method indicates what its internal strengths and weaknesses, external threats and opportunities are. To aim achieve its planning strategic plan every year. Before the organization is not technological innovation, it can't have control is looking ahead, due to planning is looking back because organization can;t know what it's mission and objectives can't achieve to revise if it has no any strategic plan, operational plan and tactical plan for top, middle and low level to let different department managers to know what it's mission and objectives are planned to achieve before the organization has not changed the technological innovation of organizational structure in the year. Besides, after the technological innovation changed the organizational structure. The management needs to concern how to implement it's strategies effectively. The technological innovation of organization needs to change its old long term strategic plan to be new long term strategic plan in the top level, e.g. one year what is its new mission for its technologcial innovation, e.g. Apple brand of computer company needs to innovate its old style computer design to know how to adapt the young client group needs (demand) in this competitive computer technological product industry.

Finally, after innovative organizational structure, mangement needs to concern how to raise skillful labor individual productivity and efficiency, due to who need to increase more effort to do their jobs after technological innovation. I shall indicate on job training method. The advantages on limitations of different approaches to on the job training include the company needs to spend extra time and resources to train staffs or workers to work, when who are on the regular work time. Hence, it will lose staffs to do regular job duties, due who needs to learn how to do their job. So the employer needs to pay higher salary to every job trainer for long term if it needs to train many skillful labor after technological innovation. It can't ensure whether the training employees can work efficiently and know who are not the right staffs to get training. Hence, it will employ the staffs who are not right staffs to accept job training riskly if the mangement have not evaluate who have effort to be train to raise whose productivity and testing personal effort of evaluation is more important to the job trainers.

14 What are the (AI) technical change as exogenous or endogenous production of factor?

Finally, I shall indicate what the change is as exogenous or endogenous factor in the (AI) production function model to cause innovative technology to produce new technological product in manufacture industry. Although, economic theory firstly treated technology change is as a residual, the unexplained part remaining after the contribution of an increased quantity and quality of capital, labor and natural resources in output growth have been accounted for. However, the theory of economic growth reconsidered recently the nature of technological change and the concept of knowledge. Therefore, the new growth economic theory includes research and development is as a factor of influence in the macroeconomic models.

The endogenous or exogenous nature of technological change refers to its source: endogenous is internal to the national economy, being created by domestic private or public enterprise, when exogenous change is external originating from foreign sources. So, it seems research and development workforce is as new factor in the production function model. Although, technological progress, managerial improvements and innovation in general are nowadays largely regarded as key contributors to economic growth. Schumpeter (1939) defines technical progress in terms of production function, which describes the way the production output varies according to the quantity and quality of the input factors. So, the technological change represents the factor that shifts the production function.

From the theoretical viewpoint, it has difficult to separate knowledge from the other factors of the production function. The total labor factor productivity is usually estimated by output the capital and labor factors, weighted by their specific shares. Under perfect competition, the price of the production factors is equal to their marginal productivity, hence, their shares in outputs are equal to their exponents from the production function.

Otherwise, from the empirical point of view, there are difficulties of measurement, especially in the case of value added and research-development variables. So, from all available data on research and development input and outputs, research and development expenditures are most frequently used, along with the number of patents, the technological balance of payments, machinery and tools inputs etc. costs to measure of input in innovation.

Furthermore, the exponents of the new growth theory indicates modeled knowledge is as an output quality of the research and development sector and proved that contrary to the neoclassical conclusions of the diminishing-returns technology, the introduction of the human capital changes the production function into one with increasing returns. Thus, it seems total research and development expenditures are used in this model as a measure of total investments (material and intangible) in the research and development sector. However, in many studies, the research and development stock is calculated as the accumulated value of research and development expenditure after depreciation, a procedure which implies the assumption that all of the research and development expenditure certainly and that it's stock depreciates with a certain fixed rate. Since, long time-series data on R & D are rarely available, other studies assume that the growth rate of R & D expenditure to R & D stock is stable. Hence in innovation technological industry, the labor production factor can be divided into two components total employees population outside the research development sector and the number of employees in research and development. The same types of division was applied to the capital production factor.

Reference

Christensen, C.M. (2003) " the innovator's dilema", Harpercollins, New York.

Davila, T., Epstein, M. J., Shelton.R. (2006) " Making innovation work: How to manage it, measure it and profit from it". Warton school publishing, New Jersey.

Schmookler, J., (1962) " Economic sources of incentive activity, " the journal of economic history. vol. 22 , no. 1 (Mar. 1962), 1-20.

Schumpeter, J., A. (1939), business cycles: A Theoretical Historical And Statistical Analysis Of Capitalist Processes, New York: Macmillan.

Reference
Future of jobs survey, World Economic Forum.
Hauser, J. Tellis, G. J; Griffin, A. 2006. Research On Innovation: A Review And Agenda For Marketing Science. 25(6): 687-717.
J.P. Holdren & P.R. Enrlich, " Human population and the global environment", American Scientist, vol. 62 (1974), pp.282-92.
Joel E. Cohen, How many people can the earth support? (New York: Norton, 1995), pp. 212-36, 261-62.
Mohr, G. J. Griffin, A. 2010. Research On Innovation : A Review And Agenda For Marketing Science. 25 (6): 687-717.
Names of drivers have abbreviated to ensure legibility.
Future of jobs survey, World Economic Forum.
" Presence to prosperity", PWC Growth Markets Centre Report: http://www.pwc.com/gx/en/growth-markets-centre/presence-to-profitability.jhtml

● How to let passengers feel impact of undergrouund train transport to their
working time efficiency

Any countries must need road, sea and air transport to assist businessmen to transport products in local or overseas. If the country's road , sea or air transport system service quality is poor. It will influence any products transport time, speed, inefficient transport to anywhere. How to raise the country's transport system in order to improve efficiencies to let any businessmen can deliver their products to anywhere easily,e.g. warehouses, client homes, supermarkets destination in the most short time to avoid delay occurrence to let clients feel unsatisfactory or complaint their perform their delivery services poorly.

I shall discuss the factors how to improve any countrues' transport systems to achieve the most efficient way as below:

Any countries‘ transport systems will create economic value, e.g. demonstrate value for money, economic worth, viable commercial worth, financial affordable worth, achieveable worth. Any countries' transport systems can bring welfare value by economics. It has direct relationship to take the form of measured economic activity, i.e. GDP. The form of measured economic activity can impact on any countries‘ economic economic geography, locally , regionally and nationally's local GDP impacts. The welfare impacts may include: leisure time savings, e.g. the local people drive cars or catch any public transportation tools to go to any geogrpahical location's shopping centers, big gardens, swimming pools, cinemas etc. places to carry on any kinds of leisure activities.

Environmental impacts may include avoiding noise, air pollution on road transportation aspect , when the main road is only on on focus on the main city,

but the city lacks other roads to let any drivers can choose them to drive, instead of the main road in the city. Then, when many cars are driven on the busy transport

time, e.g. morning working time or night busy time between 6:00 and 9:00 AM, between 6:00 and 9:00 PM. When either many working people need to catch public transport or drive themselves cars to go to offices to work or they need to catch pubic transport tools or drive themselves cars to home. Then, the only one main road problem will need them to stay themselves cars on roads, due to traffic jam or traffic accidence occurrence problem causes when many cars are driven on the road in the busy transport time. It will influence they can not go to offices or homes easily daily, even in the busy transport time, their cars' gas need to be used much to cause air pollution and traffic noise is easily caused easily in the busy transport time on the road. When the city has only one main road for drivers in the busy transport time. So, poor road transport system can bring poor impact on economic welfare benefits arising from proved labour supply from commuting, time savings, including exchequer benefits. Consequently, the county's GDP will be fallen down, due to labour market effects which do not add to welfare value.

Whether can poor transport system impact indirectly on GDP or not on local, regional , or national economic geography impacts? Does transport lead to greater economic activity i.e. higher GDP? DO they lead to change in economic activity location? Does transport impact the existence of business location and new economic activity opportunities? The measurement on every country's transport how impacts on economic change, facilitating geographic division of labour and specialization. It can be analyzed on these general aspects:

Costs and speed of travel time (Economic value of travel time savings) . Travel time savings to users from improved transport is a key of economic value, but it has only less influence,journey time reliability is more important to business frieght as well as business travellers, network connectivity enhancements as well as business travellers, network connectivity enhancement can help people and goods travel more quickly (i.e. linked to jounrey time and journey time reliability, as well as opening new destinations and new journeys, comfort and quality service provision is relevant to public transport, e.g. detering jounreys at particular times or by certain modes (e.g. overcrowding), impact on productivity at work for commuters, safety and security , due to loss of output from workers, transport accidents occur easily. All of these issues will impact any countries‘ standard of living to local people (geography) , even GDP income.

Why does the direct and indirect effects of transportation have a positive impact on the economic growth and development of a country? Does it influence acccess to goods, services and
employment opportunities in any regions? Underdeveloped countries must need to consider how transport system influences their economic growth. For example, the costs of transportation and production are reduced through timely delivery and enhancing the economies of scale in the production process, when the road is often traffic joam, gas cost, time waste , air pollution cost, noise has many roads, but if one lorry drivers needs drive more than one day to day to deliver goods to another city's warehouse every day. It will bring psychological pressure in terrible, when they need long time to drive on the road. They can not sleep easily because road accident will occur easily when they need to spend long time to drive lorries on the road.

So, how to solve the long driving time on road transport problem will be one issue concerns human life welfare benefit aspect, instead of economic benefit aspect. The transport system welfare worth needs to include human life worth. It is a valuable insight into the causality (ot lack of causality) between transport and economic growth and will serve to compare to any countries' national level and local geographical location level both.

In special, underdeveloped countries‘ public transport time whether it is long or short factor, it will influence workers their going to offices to work time. If they often need spend long time to catch buses, due to traffic jam,then it will influence their efficiences to be reduced, productive number is influenced to reduce also, because traffic jam causes they often go to offices too lately.It can influence workers' bad emotion to work every day. So, traffic jam will bring negative relationship between low efficiency and bad emotion to the workers, because they need to spend long time to wait, public transportation tools and traffic jam also influence their working emotion. Consequently, service and working performance will be influenced to poor, because long time traffic jam problem causes their bad emotion to work. It is one critical factor in the path of more widely spread economic growth and urbanization for traffic jam problem to underdeveloped countries.

However, transport system can also influence developed countries' economy. How does it influence on environmental impacts aspect from mature stage. Its business activities must raise, dramastic expansion during this period, such as underdeveloped country, US, UK. In order to acheive long term sustainable development , new demands are being placed on transport sector, such as underground mass transit rail transport , ferry, local air frieght transport, train , e.g. Japan, Fance, US high speed prior rail. Because their developed countries , business and entertainment activities needs increase, it influences high time efficient and rapid speed public transportation tools needs are also needed in societies. These new technological public transport tools invention will impact on climate, noise, human health, land use and damage to ozene layer, acidification aspects, instead of economic beneficial aspect. For long -term sustainable development to be achieved, the various activities within developed and underdeveloped societies must be adapted to what can be tolerated by humans and by the natural environment. Transport is an activity which affects humans and the natural environment for both the development of society as a whole as well as for the mobility for the individual. For Swedish underdeveloped country example, air pollution in Swedish urban areas has beed reduced, but in many places concentrations of certain substances deiving from transport activities are still at unacceptable levels and much more has to be done. Carbon dioxide emissions and noise are examples of environmental problems demanding further efforts. Measures to limit the exploitation of valuable natural and cultural environments to protect biological diviersity are also needed. So, if Swedish still hopes to develop its tourism industry to attract many travellers to choose to travel itself country. It needs to solve environmental problems from different modes of transport are of different dimensions, such as improving its air transport to avoid cause different problems and rail transport differs in turn from road transport.

The transport problem to Swedish may include poor technological communication information to its public and purchasers of transportation and communication services as to the environmental effects of different solutions is significant in creating the demand for environmentally sound public transport service concepts. It is therefore important that such lacking high technological communication and information system is presented in as completem accurate and clear way as a method for non-monetary comparison of the environmental public transport service system aspect.

In real, it's public tranport service system is needed to be improved and upgraded in order to let travellers feel Swedish's any rail, underground train, ferry, bus , taxi etc. different public transport travelling service can provide excellent performance to serve their travelling passengers, when they need to catch any kinds of public transport tools to go to travel. They can feel convenient and comfortable to attract them to visit Swedish to travel again. Then, its tourism industry GDP income will be raised, if Swedish government can innovate any new kinds of purchase ticket equipment to install in and public transport stations to let travelling passengers feel that they do not need to spend long time to queue to buy tickets to catch ferry, train, underground mass transit rail on stations conveniently. Because long time purchase ticket queue waiting will cause travellers feel its public service performance dissatisfaction and they will complain , even they won't choose to catch the kind of public transport, even the travellers won't choose to travel Swedish again, if they feel Swedish is one developed country, but it neglects to take care about travellers' catching public transport travelling service needs.

It is one poor or bad feeing to let travellers choose to Swedish again. Hence, Swedish needs to improve its public transport service performance in order to achieve to raise their comfortable and satisfactory catching public transport tools needs to let travellers to feel. They may include efficient land use for transportation tools, comprising issues concerning natural and cultural environment, natural resources, biological diversity and aesthetics, noise reducing, public transportation energy consumption and time consumption reducing, raising public transport service facilities performance functions and other issues concerning the model. For example, Swedish government can facilitate the public transport price conparison and journey time spending comparison information gathering enquiring machines public transportation selection method of public transportation services to let every travellers can evaluate different modes of public transport when they are staying in ferry, bus, train, underground mass transit rail, taxi stations.

A travelling family can seek its sustainable transport selection system for passenger transport tool. When they touch the enquiry machine, they can compare busm ferry, train, underground train, taxi price and journey spending time from their transportation stations to another destinations. Then, travelling passengers can compare these public transport tools ticket prices, journey spending time immediately when they touch the public transport enquiring machines in stations any time. Then, they can make the most righ choice to decide whether they ought catch which kind of public transport tool to arrive the another journey destination. It is one every attractive high technological enquiry method to help any travelling passegners to choose which kind of public transport tool, it can be the most cheap transport tool at the moment in any public transport stations. So , for developed countries innovative its public transport service performance will need future passengers‘ journey needs daily. Hence, they can not neglect how to improve public transport service needs to satisfy passengers to feel satisfaction, if Sweden government hopes its tourism industry can raise GDP income in long time.

- How underground train MTR can let passengers to feel catching time reducing

It has close relationship between globalization and global tranport development. How globalisation impacts on the environment via changes taking place in the transport sectors. In fact, it is not clear how the relative price changes that result from openness will affect the environental composition of economic activity. For example, some countries will produce more environmentally intensive goods, others will produce fewer. On the other hand, liberalisation will raise incomes, perhaps increasing the willingness to pay for environmental improvement. These potential income effects increased outweigh the negative scale effects with increased economic activities. When combined with the positive effects with technology transfer, the net effect on local pollutants could be positive . Hence, we need to find methods to solve the problem of raising transport economic activities and serious environmental pollution creating as the same time occurrence.

Globalisation helps to facilitate greater division of labor, and to exploit its comparative advantage more completely. In longer term, globalization also stimilates technology an dlabour transfers, and allows the dynamism that accompanies economic activities to stimulate the development of new transport technologies and short time transport processes that lead to global welfare improvement.

On shipping transport industry aspect, shipping will increase ocean pollution, when international shipping activities are increasing. Trade and shipping encourages energy use in shipping is coupled with the movement of waterborne commerce. The estimates depending on the transport goods number of at-sea or in port days much increase globally every day. The energy demand of international shipping fuel sale number and domestically assigned fuel sales number also increases for global fuel usage. Estimates of ocean going ships now consume about 2% to 3% and perhaps even as much as 4% of world fossil fuels.Hence, when global shipping energy fuel usage number increases, because global shipping trading activities number increases. It will bring the environmental pollution to ocean level increases.

On air transport industry aspect, their travellers' catching air plans travelling needs and businesses' goods transport air delivery service needs are increasing from the requirements for high quality , fast and reliable international transport. Moreover, the networks that airline companies operate have changed often to hub-and spoke networks, many new often low -cost companies have entered the air freight market, any long time air journey is needed, e.g. Australia airline expands its one new air journey flies to UK, it needs two days flying time. It means that every flight to UK from Australia , it needs to use more fuel to fly. Then , air pollution will increase also.

On road transport industry aspect, global road transport cost and transit times, traffic jam occurrence chances also increase because when the road building number is increasing globally. So, it will cause traffic jam and long journey time spending , even fuel usage spending number is also increased. Then, accident occurrence chance is raised. Hence, global business or entertainment transport activities number increasing , it will bring much negative impact on environmental pollution, traffic jams number increases, long journey spending time increases, fuel usage number increases. Although , frequent transport activities may bring GDP income.

On transport service industy aspect, but is also brings negative influence to standard of living. It means that when transport fuel demand increases, transport activities number increases, GDP income on relative any transport activities needs industy , e.g. logistic demand needs, when lorry drivers need to drive lorries to deliver goods from one warehouse to another warehouse or supermarket or office etc. different business places on the road driving activities increase. But, it also bring air pollution , traffic noise and traffic jam etc. transport problems to road and natural environment and raises worse standard of living , bad emotion to working people or learning emotion to students , due to frequent traffic jam causes , low efficiency and productivity to workers, even student individual learning time can be reduced if they need to spend long time to wait bus, ferry, rail, underground train to go to schools , due to frequent long time traffic jam occurs on the roads to influence they can not go to schools on time often when they are catching buses to go to schools absolutely in busy transport time.

Thus, although any countries need to consider how to design their transport system, e.g. how to e.g. how to choose the right locations to build roads to let many cars can be driven available easily when the morning and evening (office and school transport busy time, e.g. 6:00 to 9:00 AM morning, 6:00 to 9:00 PM in the evening transport time usually because these two transport periods are usually , there are many students and working people need to catch any public transportation or drive cars tools to go back homes. So, enough roads number and long and not narrow road area must be needed to design in order to let enough cars be driven on the roads in the transport busy times to the countries have many big cities or have high population , such as UK, US, China, India, Hong Kong. They have many people , but drivers and cars numbers both are increasing. So, efficient road design and road number are also needed to increase in order to let drivers can transport goods to deliver, students and working people can catch any public transport tools to arrive any destinations on reads in the short time rapidly in order to avoid to spend long time transportation time and late to arrive any destinations in possible occurrence. So, any sudden traffic jam is not hoped to be caused by easy traffic accidents occurrence any time.

Hence, global efficient road transport system is needed, when global transport activities are increased, because any road logistic transport activities are increasing, they will also influence the students and working people when they also need to catch any public transport tools or drive themselves cars to go to working places or schools on the roads at the same busy transport time between 6:00 to 9:00 AM morning busy transport time and between 6:00 to 9:00 PM evening busy transport time. Because these both times will be have many students, working people , they need either go to offices or schools or go to homes. Hence, if the country had many lorry drivers need to drive their lorries to deliver goods on the roads in the transport busy morning or evening time in the same driving time on the roads. It will increase the risk to cause frequent traffic jam or traffic accident occurrence easily in possible in the country. So, any countries' governments can not neglect how to design roads and choose anywhere are the roads suitable locations to be built as well as anywhere land useful number to build road location choices in order to solve geographical traffic jams occurrence chance.

Hence, globalization of transport activities may bring geographical GDP growth, but it also bring traffic jams and traffic accidents occurrences, hearing impairment due to traffic noise, air pollution, traffic crashed, bad working emotions to workers and bad learning emotions to students, due to spending long transport time when traffic jam or traffic accidence occurs more easily.

However, transportation is an important tool if a country's progress. Rapid economic growth and increasing level of urbanization enhances a person's living standard have, it leads to a greater travel demands. Hence, governments ought not neglect have to design its roads , measure every road's length or width whether it has how many cars need to drive in morning or evening transport busy time for students, working people and delivery goods drivers of public transportation tools or private transportation tools easy driving needs in order to avoid frequent traffic jams or traffic accidents occurrences in possible.

Moreover, any governments also need to solve these issues, if they hope to develop their transport system successfully. These issues include : What mode of transportation to cost-effective in meeting a region's transportation needs to the country? How should a state department of transportation prioritize its highway delivers to maximize economic growth? What is the trade-off between additional growth in urban area and the cost of expanding transportation systems to accommodate greater growth? What effect does the expansion of transportation systems have on the need to invest in other types of transport modes? For example , the transport expansion may include the construction of additional highway segments, rail lines, runways, or additional sea, air, rail or bus terminal capacity using traditional technology; highway may include the additional of lanes to an interstate highway system; the conversion of an existing two-lane road to a four lane limited access highway, replacement or widening of bridges, and the extension of an existing road. Airport examples, include runway lengthening, apron expansion, and additional terminal gates.

On the other hand, enhancement to new transport technologies may bring efficiency of the existing highway system, examples may include intelligent highway systems, congestion pricing, intermodal freight facilities, geographic positioning systems, and instrument landing systems to mention of a few major transport innovations. So, transport policy makers need to understand the effects of these new transport mode innovations on economic development or GDP growth on transport activities growth transportation services and a more efficient use of limited land supplying scarce resources , air quality ,and noise pollution, traffic jams, long spending transport time to students, working people, entertaining people, even deliver goods lorry drivers their every day essential driving activities or catching public transportation tools needs problems. For example, the concept of intelligent highway systems needs increase trend. In simply , vehicles are being linked to each other and to traffic control devices to improve the efficiency of the total highway system. Similar types of innovations in intelligent traffic management are increasing needs for air, sea, and rail systems. The question is that whether intelligent highway systems can attribute of highways on economic development, raising on productivity of reducing highway congestion or improving pavement condition.

In fact, many developed countries' transportation system is mature. The nation has gone beyond the frontier of building, the interstate highway system and connecting most cities (markets). Tweaking the system with additional lanes and the new intelligent highway systems are useful in China, US, UK, because they have many cities. SO, road efficient traffic congestion control is needed when many students, working people, delivery goods transport people need to drive cars or catch cars on every city's roads in the transport busy time between 6:00 to 9:00 AM morning transport busy time as well as between 6:00 to 9:00 PM evening transport busy time.

However, transportation investment must be needed, if the country hoped to have good economic productivity, efficient transport service can bring good effects on the flows goods and people on roads every day when they use the country's transport system. So, any countries need to collect data, they can not be lack of enough transport information in any time that links anywhere locations of any drivers to the locations of the transport system that provide them with services in any time, e.g. every day morning and evening transport busy time, radio can report the real transport time of any roads traffic jam or traffic accident message to let drivers to listen to know whether anywhere roads are occurring traffic accidents or traffic jams or when the road traffic accident or traffic jam is solved to let the drivers can know whether when the roads can be opened to drive again. So, real time road transport message information is needed to report by radio, in order to let any drivers to know whether they ought choose to drive themselves cars on the road when they need to choose anywhere road to drive to the destination if they can know when the road has traffic accident or traffic jam occurs. They won't drive their cars on the road in the moment immediately.

On conclusion, globalization can being frequent transport economic activities. So, road , air, sea, transport service users' transport service needs are also increased. Every country ought not neglect how to innovate their transport service in order to satisfy their transport needs to achieve economic growth, efficient and short transport time spending, productivities increase, reducing air pollution, traffic noise , raisins standard of living on transport influence aspect to satisfy working people, students, entertaining people, delivery goods transport users' efficient road transport time behavioral spending aspect.

Artificial intelligent public transport how influences passenger psychology

How technology influence passenger psychology

Nowadays, robotic invention can be applied to factory manufacture, hotel, restaurant, shopping center, customer service, accounting, law document draft etc. general office tasks aspect, evem hospital surgen patient medical operation health service aspects. If future robotic non -manual driving vehicles can be invented to reach the safe auto driving mature skill stage. Any one driver begins to believe robotic, driving safe level is bette than he/she drives himself/herself car. I assume that if future robotic public transport tool drivers can replace human public transport tool drivers to drive bus, taxi, train, tram, ferry, underground train, tram , even air plane ets. different kinds of public transport tools. How non maual driving public transport tools influence our social change either to improve better ot worse? How non manual driving public transport tools influence passenger psychology, e.g. increasing any kinds of public transport tools passengers safe feeling to choose to catch any kinds of public transport tools to go to anywhere or feeling more dangerous when the passenger himself/herself chooses to sit the non manual driving public transport tool.

In past, traditional public transport tools are driven by human drivers, if one day non manual driving skills are invented to reach the most safe level, when the car owner or passenger is sitting on the non manual driving vehicle or public transport tool, the artificial intelligent driver can help the driver to control the car wheel to avoid to crash any other cars or pedestrians to o to any far places on the roads easily. The public bus does not human driver to drive the bus, artificial intelligent driver won't feel tried, when it drives the bus long time, it does not need to leave the bus to go to toilet, to go to restaurant to eat, to go to rest room for rest, because it is one (AI) machine. So, the (AI) driver won't have negative emotion to feel angry when the bus passenger complaints its service is poor when he feels dissatisfactory to the (AI) driver bus service performance.

However, human bus driver may be complainted for unpolite or rude bus service attitude. It is common human bus driver will encounter any unreasonable passenger complain in general . Hence, when non manual driving technology can be invented to reach the most safe driving skill level, whether (AI) machine driver is the most suitable to replace any public transport tool drivers, such as bus, taxi, train, underground train, ferry, tram, even air plane to drive for future passengers service need.

In fact, any public transport tool drivers may cause traffic transport accidents, due to their careless driving to crash any other vehicles or pedestrians (walling people). Consequently, any passengers may have chance to be killed by public transport tool crashing accident. So, it seems that global public transport tools are dangerous to any passengers, when they are sitting on the bus, taxi, train, tram, underground train road public transport tools, or ferry sea public transport tools, because any human public transport tool drivers will feel tried to drive any one kind of public transport tool long time, for example when the bus driver has no enough nervous to drive the bus, he wants to sleep, due to he often needs to follow night time bus timetable to drive bus long time at night. When he often want to sleep and he is driving the bus, traffic accidents will be caused easily. So, any passenger individual life is dominated by the sleeping bus driver. His bus dirving behavior is not safe to any one bus passenger when the bus passegner chooses to catch this feeling sleeping bus driver's bus to catch.

Otherwise, (AI) non manual driver must not feel tried or need sleep often. It is one automative driving mature, it can drive any kinds of public transport tools all day, because (AI) machine drivers do not need sleep, (AI) none human auto-driving driver can bring this important unique benefit to any kinds of public transport tools to compare human drivers. Instead of (AI) automatic driving tools' non need sleeping advantage, (AI) non-manual control auto-driving tools must not own sad, disappointing feeling , tried feeling, anygry emotion feeling when it needs to contact angry passengers every day. So, I mean that any traffic accident occurrence will reduce, when (AI) drivers often feel happy to drive any kinds of public transport tools. Otherwise, any human public transport drivers will be influenced to feel angry when they are complaint by angry passenger in any driving time easily. So, public transport traffic accident will be caused to occur easily. Althoug, it is not guarantee that it is obsolute none any public transport accident occurrence, due to crash to other vehicles, during the non manual driving (AI) driver drives the bus, tram, train, taxi, on the road, nut when (AI) non manual driving skill can be improved to the most safe driving level. I believe that non manual driving public transport tools ought be bring more safe to compare human public transport tools drivers to any one passenger individual life safety.

How non manual driving automated vehicle influences future mode of public transport service change? A survey distributed in the Netherlands in which respondents had to choose between conventional cars, public transportation for different travel distances and trip purposes. having collected information from 663 respondents, conducted a study on classic trip attributes (such as travel time, car owner self driving time and non manual driving public transport tool driving time as well as travel costs, car owner car fuel purchase expenditure and general non manual driving public transport tool fare comparison), attitudinal factors and socio-economic variables to understand future non manual auto driving public transport tools choices. The repor indicates that automated driving transport service which they defined as an automatically controlles door-to-door transport service provided by a vehicle with similar features to a conventional car, albeit driveless. Results suggest that travellers' mode preferences vary significantly for different travel distances and purposes. They found that conventional cars and public transportation are perceived as being the least attraction altererernatives in relation to vehicle travel time and short -and -long distance commuting trips respectively, preference for passegner choice is between the non-manual driving auto car and non manual driving auto public transport tool.

They indicated that future passengers will consider how non-manual driving public transport tools whether they can bring trips are safer, faster and more efficient to let them to feel as well as traveling time and time cost is also another factor to influence them to choose to catch non-manual driving public transport tool, when they feel safe to arrive the destination rapidly. Then, future many passengers will be persuaded to choose to catch non-manual auto driving public transport tools in preference. So, if future all public transport service providers can let passengers to feel fares are reasonable price, when their non-manual driving public service transport tools, bus, taxi, tram, train, underground train etc. they can let them to feel safe to arrive destinations rapidly, they won't need worry about passengers number will reduce when human drivers are replaced by AI robotic drivers.

In fact, when one needs to drive to arrive destination in long driving time. The car owner will feel tried, bored and he/she can not spend driving time to do his/her interesting activites in his/her car, e.g. reading, listening music, watching TV, playing electronic games from smartphone, phone talking etc. personal behaviors. So, it means that future long time trip passengers may be persuaded to catch non-manual auto driving public transport tools if they believe that this kind of new non manual auto driving pubic transport tools can provide more safe, efficient, rapid, comfortable feeling to them, when they are sitting on them. All of these may be the main factors to influence them to choose to catch non -manual auto driving public transport tools. In general, these other factors may influence future passengers to choose to catch non manual auto driving public transport tools, they may include: whether automated vehicle would drive on populated streets better than conventional cars, whether an automated car would be comfortable entrusting the safety of a close family member, whether automated vehicle might produce fewer pollutant emissions. Because , when future non-manual auto driving vehicles are popular, many car owners will choose to buy automated vehicles to drive. So, future non manual auto driving public transport tool service providers

, their competitors may be automated vehicles. If automated vehicles can let car owners to feel car prices are reasonable, they can provide safe, rapid speed, comfortable feeling to any one car owner, then he/she can sell his/her traditional car to change new automated car easily, when global many car owners begin to accept automated cars.

On conclusion, future passengers may be persuaded to choose to buy fares to catch any kinds of non manual auto driving public transportation tools. It depends on these factors, such as reasonable fares, safe feeling, efficient and rapid arriving to destinations short time journey, comfortable and clean seats facility, free personal behavior, e.g. quite reading , listening music, watching TV , free internet provision transport environment, when future any one passenger is sitting in the auto driving public transport vehicle. So, (AI) technology will have possible to influence our future social public transportation development may bring more significant new travelling experiences and it can let global passengers to feel indeed. Moreover, it will be future global public transportation service providers, they need to consider that they ought need to change their public transport tools services in order to satisfy future passengers transport needs more easily. I conclude that future global public transport service will be influenced to change non manual auto driving public transport services by future global passegner public transport service needs within 10 years. So, nowadays, any kinds of public transport service providers ought need to spend time to research how to design themselves traditional public transport service moods to change to non manual auto driving moods in order to satisfy future global passenger individual new public transport services needs successfully.

TWO

FUTURE TRANSPORT NEED CHANGE TO DEVELOPED COUNTRIES

How future our transport need change? What factors influence our future transport need change? In general, these factors may influence our transportation need change. They may include fuel cost, the labor market for commercial drivers, demand for frieight , customer loyalty , vehicle capacity, government regulation, geographical events, the public transport tool reputation to passegners as a merchant. However, the factors that influence the development of transport system in an area? They may include as below:

Environment at the local scale existing hydrographical and geomorphological characteristics are string, factors in transport development, particularly in terms of the technical challenges (bridge, gradients,) they present to construct, other factors may include historical, technological, political and economic factors. All of these factors may influence our future transport system how develops. For raiway development influential factors, they may include: Geograohical factors, e.g. the North Indian plain with its level land, high density of population and rich agriculture presents the most favourable conditions for the development of railways in India. However, the presence of large number of rivers makes it necessary to construct bridges which involve heavy expenditure to Indian Government publich transport expenditure.

How transport has changed from past to present?

There has been a remarkable development in modern transportation. The stream engine and then the stream trains have emerged and spread at this time and in abundance until the discovery of natural gas and oil was an evolution of transportation. Thus, the sedams and vehicles began to run in oil, until present battery changes energy vehicle need, even future non-manual driving artificial intelligent driving vehicle need. These new transport technology may influence our future public transportation from gas energy to battery changed energy, even non-manual driving vehicles need to our daily transport need.

So, our future purpose of public transport need is the unique purpose to oversome space, which is shaped by a variety of human and physical constraints, such as distance, time. These both is our future main public transport need main purpose factors, short distance and reducing journey time, they influence that why we need to choose to catch any kinds of public transportation tool to replace purchase private cars to drive transport tool choice. So, future any kinds of public transport tools, they need to consider above both main factors , how to attract passengers to choose to catch themselves public transport tools choice in this competitive public transport tools market.

On the other hand, the economic importance of transportation development can be defined as improving the welfare of a society, through appropriate social, political and economic conditions , such as US Government spent too much money to assist MTR (MAss transport railway firm) to develop underground thrain transport. Its aim to let many passegner can reduce journey time and reduce distance between destinations, it also hopes US citizen passengers can pay cheap transport fare to buy ticket to catch underground transport train for many families their transport expenditure in social transport welfare view.

However, US Government neds to solve those challenges, before it implements to develop rapid underground railway , e.g. lack of knowledge of geographical fwatures, lack of manpower necessary to operate the rapid underground railway construction work, lack of construction materials within the US itself. For Brazil rail network transportation development example, the factors influence the use of rail network for transportion is highly restricted in Brazil. Thus, the development of roadways and waterways is the main modes of transportation that caould be used in Brazil given its topography and drainage benefit to society . So, brazil can develop rail network for transportation development in success.

So, transportation system is important in the development of any nation, because transportation plays important role in rapid economic growth of a nation. Thrapsortation increases the quality and variety of consumer goods, thereby stimulating the demand and development of trade and economy of the nation. Moreover, transport provides various employment opportunities and boosts up the economy of the country.

Also, any transport tools need to improve themselves transport service in order to attract passengers to choose their public transport service more easily. They may attempt to sign up for an autonomous vehicle pilot program, free phone enquiey concerns whether the passegner can catch which bus bumber to go to the destination, hou much bus fare, how long journey time, when the bus will arrive teh bus stops or leave the bus stop etc. bus service questions, before any one passenger prepares to choose to catch bus (free bus go phone call enquiry), free download a public transport tool transit app. even water taxi tranport tool innovation can replace ferry public transport tool, it can let passengers have more fun an enjoyable catching feeling. So, water taxi tranport tool is one kind of future new transport tool change to replace ferry , it can influence ferry passengers to choose water taxi public transport tool to replace ferry. Although, its fare may be more expsnse to compare ferry, but it can reduce jounrey time and distance between both water stations, when ferry can not arrive the other destinations, but water taxi can arrive any one water station destination. It can bring convenient to future any one ferry passengers. So, water taxi may be developed to some countries, e.g. New Zealand , Auckland city, US , Washington and New York cities they had developed water taxi public transport tools to let ferry passengers have one kind new water public transport choice.

However, instead of new transport innovation improvement to water transport service public transport with input from the public on bus transport service aspect, bus frequency improvement, it means when booking at ways to improve, bus frequency from long times to less times, efficient bus ticketing system, a big part of how to improve tranportation efficiency is improving transit ticketing system.

In fact, my future transport system may still include these five types, modes of transport are: railway, roadways, airways, waterways and piplelines. Also, among different includes of transport, railways are the different modes of transport, railways are the cheapest. Trains cover the distance in less time and comparatively, the fare is also less to other modes of transporation. Therefore, railways is the cheapest mode of transportation to compare ferry, water taxi , sea transport, bus, taxi, road system.

On conclusion, transport price is not the main factor to attract passegners to choose to catch. The importance to have a good public transport system in place. It may be one main factor to help the kind of public transport tool to attract passengers to choose to catch, because a good transport links can widen people's job search area and help them find employment. It can also reduce commuting times and reduce the cost of living, and high skilled workers are more likely to travel across longer distances to work, especially if they are following good job opportunities. So, future any one kind of public transportation tool service provider ought consider how to satisfy working people working time need to shorten journey time to any working places or student learning time need to shorten jounrey times to any schools as well as let they feel comfortable to sit on comfortable chairs or provide free internet service to themselves mobiles , laptops, when they are sitting down or standing up in the kind of public transport . It is the important factor to influence any kind of public transport service in success.

Future Non-Manual driving vehicle How
Influences Public Transport Tool Passenger Need

Nowadays, artifical intelligent (non-manual) driving vehicles are invented, it may be accepted to any countries families to feel comfortable to drive on roads, because any people choose to buy any kinds cars, when any people choose to buy kinds of non-manual (artificial intelligent) vehicles, they do not need to use their hands to drive cars, because artificial intelligent (robotic auto control wheels, it means that robots can help human (drivers) to control wheel to drive to avoid any cars crash occurrence on the roads more easily.

If one day, non-manual driving robotic control whoole vehicles are invented in successful, whether it will persuade many different conuntries families choose to buy non-manual (robotic auto control wheel) vehicles, then it will cause bus, tram, train, underground train, road transport need will be influenced to reduce or even if non-manula boats are invented, whether it will cause ferry sea transport needs will b influenced to reduce. Hence, future non-manual driving vehicles or bats invention whether they will influence public transport tool of road and sea transport passengers number reduces. It is one interesting question. I shall attempt to discuss as below:

In fact, non-manual vehicles are very attraction, to excite any person chooses to buy to drive, because people do not need often touch wheels and touch foots button to control cars to move often forever, when robotic can be invented to help human to control car wheel and foot button, any person only needs to sit on his/her car, then the car can move rapidly, because any drivers is lazy, he/she hopes machine can help her/him to drive car on the road safely. So, he/she can read book or listen music or eatch mobile movie to enjoy his/her entertainment when he/she is sitting on his/her car.He/she will feel more comfortable and enjoyable when robotic can help him/her to drive car. So, robotic (non -manual driving vehicle) can encourage people to choose to buy cars because any drivers won't need to drive cars, robotic can help drivers them to drive on the road easily, when global any one family can own one robotic auto control (non-manual driving) car at least, it may influence these owning non-manula diriving vehicle owners do not feel need to pay any fares to buy road public transport tools of bus ticket, train ticket, underground train ticket , tram ticket to go to anywhere. So, it seems that robotic (non-manual driving) vehicles may influence future any road transport passengers number reduces , because traditional catching any kinds of road public transport tool passengers will be influenced to choose to sit themselves auto (non-manual) driving cars to go to offices to work, parents do not need to follow their sone/daughters to sit on themselves non-manual auto driving cars to go to schools, because their sons/daughters can sit on themselves non-manual driving cars to go to schools more easily. In holidays, they can sit on themselves non-manual driving cars to go to cinemas, music halls, breachs, theaters, shopping centers, gardens different entertainment places to enjoy their any leisure safely because robotic can help them to drive their cars on roads safely.

So, it means that robotic auto control driving cars can influence global every family to feel that they do not need to catch any kinds of public transport tools, e.g. bus, train, tram, taxi underground train to go to anywhere because robotic auto driving cars can help any one, he/she does not know how to drive car to go to anywhere safely. So, future any one won't need to learn driving car skill, when he/she likes to buy one auto driving car. So, in passenger public transport need view, non-manual driving cars will influence them to feel any kinds of road public transport tools can help them to go to anywhere conveniently, because themselves non-manual driving vehicles can help them to drive cars to go to anywhere conveniently. They only need to tell robotic that where they want to go, when they sit on their non-manual driving cars, then robotic knows whether where destination, they want to go, their cars will auto move on the road immediately. It is one exciting and enjoyable ourney when the driver does not need to drive his/her car on the road. So, it seems that robotic (non-manual driving) vehicles invention may bring negative influence to any kinds of public transport tools service needs to passengers , when passengers had owned one non-manual driving car at least.

Why and how non-manual driving car owners need

raise public transport quality on travel time and fare aspects

- How non human driving behavior can be influence by non-manual driving cars

In fact, impact of automated vehicless on travel mode preference, it can bring both trip purposes and distances aim raising need to any kinds of public transport service passegners. Because of technology penetration in the transportation system, the automated vehicle is set to be a future mode of transport, it may bring negative impact to future any kinds of public transport passengers needs, in special on the potential impact of these non-manual driving automated vehicles on travel behaior negative impact to public transport passenger behavior. Automated vehicles will influence future public transportation passengers feel it can bring more short time travel distances and short trip purposes more benefit than any kinds of public transport choices, e.g. bus, taxi, ferry, train, tram, underground tram etc. road and sea public transport tools, e.g. ferry, water taxi. It means that when future any passenger feels above these any one kind of public transport tool needs to spend longer travel time on journey distance and trip to compare future automated vehicles, then they will choose to sit on automated vehicles in preference, due to automated vehicles can help global any one person needs to go to anywhere rapidly.

So, automated vehicles may replace general traditional public transport tools in possible, when they are popular accepted in societies. On the other, instead of shortening journey travel distance time, (travel time) aspect, public transport fare, travel cost will be another influential factor to influence future public transport tool passengers to choose automated vehicles to replace to catch any kinds of public transport tools.

In fact, conventional cars and public transport s are perceivd as being the least attractive alternative in relation to in-vehicle travel time on short and long distance communting trips. So , future automated vehicle drivers (non -human driving) behaviors will be likely changed to prefer this mode for long distance leisure trips rather than short distance commuting trips by automated vehicles.

In fact, advanced technologies have revolutionized many aspects of human life, include the automated vehicle transport system. Also, transport system is one of the essential development aspect to particular , such as non-manual driving automation , vehicle aims to make trips safer, faster , more efficient, automated vehicles passengers and drivers can feel enjoyable to do themselves leisure behavior , e.g. read books, listen, music, listen mobile, watch laptop movies when any one does not need to consider whether their cars are safe to be driven , even any one needs to drive the automated car, because robotic can help them to control how to automatic drive this car on the road safely.

Robotic will bring confidence to let them feel that themselves cars are moving safely on the roads . In recent years, the concept of automated driving has been introduced as on outstanding platform for the next generation of driving systems that is expected to improve safety, traffic flows efficiency, reducing traffic jams occurrence chance, avoiding traffic accidents occurrence chance, e.g. avoid to crash any one person when he/she is walking across road or crach any car is moving on the road easily, capacity, accessibility , and reducing congestion through the application of some technologies , such as vehicle to vehicle and vehicle to infrastructure communication.

So, future automated vechicles can have good driving facility systems to be installed in their cars, in order to raise safety, rapid driving speed level to let any one to feel , when they are sitting in their automated cars, e.g. using cameras, sensors, global positioning system adaptive cruise control, light detection and ranging, and advanced driver assistance system, automated vehicles can steer the vehicle and drive it automatically when passengers delegate control to a computer. Absolutely, ny replacing the driver role with an automated driving system , future one automated vehicle is able to totally free up passengers under automation levels.

So, unless future any kinds of public transport tools may apply automated robotic automated driven system replace the bus driver, taxi driver, train driver, tram driver, underground train driver to raise automated driving system service improvement level to let any one passengers to feel. Otherwise, when automated vehicles are popular to be accepted to buy in any one country in global. Then, global public tansport tool passegners number may be influenced to reduce when global any one family owns at least one automated vehicle at themselves homes .

In other words, automated vehicles can bring thes benefits to let global any one household family feels, future automated vehicles users , they can mostly behave like passengers inside the vehicle, which implies that they will be able to multitask and productive by allocating the travel time to do other activities, e.g. reading, eating, working, drinking, watching movies, listening musics, even sleeping. So, automated vechicles will motivate humans to change non-humanly driven behaviors from conventional humanly driven behavior. This non-humanly driven behavior may be one main factor to influence or encourage future any one kind of public transport passenger won't choose to pay fare to buy ticket to catch any one kind of public transport tool again, because non-manual driven behavior may hel many lazy people do not need to consdierate how to learn to drive cars skills to prepare pass any road test in order to earn the driving licnece to permit to drive cars forever. When automated vehiclesa re popular to be accepted to replace manual-driven cars in societies.

Hence, automated vehicles could potentially change the traditional human driven vehicle market to cause their manual driven cars sale buyers number reduces, when the automated vehicle buyers number increases, also they can chance globa public transport passengers behaviors to reduce to pay fares to catch any kinds of public transport tools when automated vechicles users may sit on themselves automated vehicles to go to anywhere in short time rapidly and safely in any countries.

On conclusion, future global public transport service competition is serious, because instead of global passengers had began to compare whether which kinds of public transport fares are cheaper, more safe, shortening journey time between leaving place and destination, more comfortable feeling, e.g. clean and comfortable chairs , mre free internet service facilities in order to make any one kind of catching public transport tool choice in preference. On the other hand, future automated vehicles number will increase when traditional manual driven car users begin to believe that automated vehicles can bring more safe , more comfortable, more fee- time using, more leisure satisfactory feeling, more than traditional manual driving cars. Then, when global any one household family had made choice to buy at least one automated vehice to replace themselves car(s) at home. When, they are habit to sit in themselves automated vehicles to go to anywhere, however, short or long trip . Consequently, global any one household family won't feel any kinds of public transport tools may bring personal economic saving cost, comfortable, enjoyable, free-time using benefit to compare themselves automated vehicles . It will cause global public transport tools passengers number will reduce , when many different kinds of home automatic vehicles are purchased to replace manual driving cars by global household automated vehicle users. So, in passegner transport tool choice psychological view, automatic vehicles will be possible to replace future public transport service tools. So, any public transport service providers can not neglect how to desing and improve their facilities , charge reasonable transport fare, provide more comfortable, and enjoyable sitting feeling , even applying automatic driving system to replace human drivers in order to attract passegners ' catching need choice more easily.

Non-manual driving public transport tools innovation

Why MTR underground train transportation needs to know passenger behaviour

Understanding individual passenger behaviour is essential for the design MTR transportation, because who can choose to catch bus, taxi, tram, train ferry etc. different kinds of public transportation tools. Individual traveler who decides to catch which kinds of public transportation tools, it depends on whether the public transportation tool can provide real time travel information, liking link travel time schedule. So, MTR underground train needs to understand where it has terminal to give convenience to the local living areas of time travelers to choose to catch MTR easily. Although, MTR ticket fare is one factor to influence any passengers choice. But, those other factors can also influence them to choice. e.g. MTR any terminal location of convenience, short time travelling, none crowding in busy (peak) time, MTR platform waiting arrival time, none sudden MTR engineering machines broken accident events occurrence frequently etc. different factors, any one of these factors which can influence passengers who choose to catch MTR or other kinds of transportation tools.

Why route choice can influence passenger behavioural choice

Usually, the busy time passengers will regard the route choice as a coordination problem to influence them to choose to catch which kinds of transportation tools. The route choice is as an opportunity costs to influence any busy time passengers to decide to choose to catch which kind of transportation tool which is the best right choice in the right time among of them. In the short time, for example, it seems any busy time passengers will choose to catch bus to substitute MTR underground train transportation tool, due to who feels the bus can arrive any destinations to compare other kinds of transportation tools in the most short time. However even if the MTR can either charge cheaper ticket fare to sell full day or charge discount ticket fare to sell in the busy (peak) time to compare to bus fare. It is possible that the busy time passengers will still choose to catch bus, if between the bus terminal and the another bus terminal that distance is the shorter time route to spend time to arrive destination to compare between the MTR terminal to the another MTR terminal arrival time . Also, although the busy time passengers will feel to enounter traffic jam to influence sitting or waiting bus time to be longer time in possible and who also feel MTR can avoid traffic jam problem. However, usually any busy (peak) time passengers will feel the chance of traffic jam occurrence will be less. So, the short bus route choice is more potential factor to influence the busy (peak) time passengers still to choose bus to catch.

However, if anyone wants to investigate results of day-to-day route choice which can be transferred to more realistic environment. It is necessary to explore individual behaviour in an interactive experimental set up to ensure busy (peak) time passenger transportation behavioural choice. For example, a passenger has a choice between a main road (M) and a side road (S) for travelling from (A) to (B). (M) is faster if (M) and (S) are chose by the same number of passengers. So, this method can be researched whether MTR terminal station is located at the main road (M) or the side road (S) where is more suitable to accept to passengers generally.

Why trip time reliability and
crowding factors can influence
MTR passenger choice.

Other problem is MTR busy (peak) time's crowding in public transportation occurrence of MTR underground train transportation tool is becoming a growth to concern as MTR demand growth at a busy (peak) time. To capture the MTR passengers benefits with reduced crowding from improved MTR public transport service and image. It is necessary a identify the relevant dimensions of crowding that are meaningful measures of what crowding means to MTR passengers. Two main influences on MTR model choice that are growing in relevance are trip time reliability and crowding. It represents a benefit-cost framework. In fact, MTR passengers can be willing to pay more expensive ticket fare, it MTR can avoid crowding and short and the accurate arrival trip time between terminals is reliable to occur. How to measure of MTR crowding, e.g. weighting the gap between the busy time, the standard (i.e. objective) and the perceived (i.e. subjective) metrics. We are not in a position to definitely map the two dimensions, which is a crucial requirement for translating objective improvements into equivalent subjective gains that then can be applied, willingness to pay estimates MTR ticket fares to obtain the additional MTR passenger benefits of MTR public transportation investment to any terminal stations. Because MTR crowding has a negative impact on passengers in terms of psychological on emotional distress. MTR passengers are willing to stand for up to 20 minutes of the service is fast and reliable. However crowding outweighed these benefits from a MTR passenger's perpective, experienced crowding leads a increased dissatisfaction. e.g. stress and less privacy during who needs to stand up in MTR. Due to there are no enough places to supply to them to stand up in MTR. If the MTR trip time was longer time between the passenger's terminals, who will feel more dissatisfaction and it will cause who feels whether who ought need to choose to catch other transportation tools to substitute MTR next time. e.g. bus, train, tram, ferry, taxi etc. So, from an operator's perspective, the MTR service frequency or MTR size is significantly influenced by the level of ridership, which sends a signal to respond if the monitored crowding level exceeds the benchmark standard in the busy time. e.g. in the morning time or at the night time, the students or employment people who need to go to schools or offices (working places). The locations of different places between MTR terminals and crowding are regarded as a key service attribute for MTR pubic transportation along with other factors, such as travelling time and reliability, e.g. service quality, none engineering machines are broken to cause MTR stops suddenly.

Given the increasing importance of crowding on both the disutility to existing MTR public transportation users and the influence to it. MTR passenger can choose to use either the MTR public public transportation or other public transportation. It is timely to review the MTR current measures of crowding defined by transportation authorities. MTR operators ought evaluate whether they apporpriately reflect MTR each traveler experiences and perceptions of crowding in busy (peak) time. I suggest that MTR needs to buy other underground trains to supply to the busy (peak) time passengers to let them have enough seats to sit down, so who do not need to stand up in any MTR underground trains when they catch MTR underground trains in busy time. It aims to let who are willingness to pay the estimation of reasonable ticket fares to compare the other kinds of transportation tools in the busy (peak) time.

What is the crowding difference
between train and MTR underground train.
In fact, crowding won't be happened to brother these transportation tools easily in the busy time and non busy time both. e.g. bus, taxi, train, tram, ferry. Because passengers can not choose to stand up in these transportation tools easily, due to these transportation tools have no enough areas (spaces) to let them to stand up easily . So, the crowding will be avoided to occur in these tranportation tools usually. Otherwise, MTR will have many passengers who can choose to stand up because MTR design of length is very long and it has enough areas (places) to let passengers to choose to stand up, even there have none any seats are provided to let them to sit down. So, MTR passengers will feel more dissatisfaction and crowding easily, especial in any peak (busy) time every day.

Comparing to bus, much more diverse crowding measures are defined in the passenger rail industry. For passenger, different specifications for measuring crowding are found across countries and even within a country. For example, rail crowding measures in the UK, the passengers in excess of capacity is crowding measure that applies to all London and South east operators weekday train services at a London terminus during the morning peak from 0700 to 09: 59 , and those departing during the afternoon peak from 16:00 to 18:59 (office of rail regulation 2011 year). The overall PIXC figure is considered the planned standard class capacity of each train service as well as the actual number of standard class passengers on the service at the critical point. i.e. the location on a trains of standard class passengers that surpass the planned capacity as the difference between the number of actual passengers and the capacity of the train divided by the number of passenger is within the capacity . So, it seems train and MTR underground public transportaton tools had been encountering the crowding problems in peak time, the difference in train passengers need to wait next train or more train arrival is who doesn't plan to enter the train, when who discovers the current train has no seats to provide to them to sit down in whose trip. Otherwise, MTR passengers can choose either to stand up within the large areas (places) if who discovered there are no any seats to provide to them to sit down or who can wait the next MTR arrival in order to who can sit down. It seems MTR transportation tool crowding environment includes in waiting platform and inside of the MTR underground train. Otherwise, train transportation tool crowding environment only includes the waiting platform and the passengers will not have crowding feeling inside of the train, due to none of passengers choose to stand up inside any trains because any train inside has no enough places to let them to stand up.

How MTR can attract many passengers.
On the commuter departure time choice of any reference point researching hand, the departure time decisions of communters are of fundamental importance of peak period MTR traffic congestion. However, whether on the demand side, MTR underground train congestion relief measures, such as MTR ticket fare to every terminal station needs to be charged cheaper fare or discount fare in the peak (busy) time every day. To aim to attract many passengers to choose to catch MTR Underground train public transportation tools, substitute to choose other public transportation tools in the peak time.

Over the past decades, there have been very active research efforts in the departure time problem, both in econometric modeling and dynamic user equilibrium fields. Although, these works provide valuable insights into dynamic commuter decision making, they do not identify the commuters' response to gains and losses related to whole actual arrival time to reference points who may have relative. The appliability of the reference point hypothesis of prospect theory to the commuter's departure time decision making to obtain a better understanding of how departure time choice in MTR platform during their waiting underground train arrival time. However, every MTR underground train actual arrival time and deviation variables related to reference points (gains and losses) are the key factors in the departure time choice model. How the MTR underground train of every communter's daily departure time decision can be modelled when the reference point hypothesis of prospect theory. The MTR underground train's schedule delay is defined as the difference between the preferred arrival time (PAT) and the actual arrival time (AT) for a given MTR communter. In a daily MTR commute, a commuter in the indifference band actual arrival time is an essential feature of MTR schedule study. Two reference points are the earliest acceptable arrival time and the work starting time for a given MTR platform waiting passengers. In psychological view point, prospect theory proposes that the displeasure of a loss is perceived or greater than the pleasure of a gain of the same attitude and therefore, the value function is stronger for losses than gains.

To conclude, it seems that if MTR waiting passengers need not spend long time to wait underground train arrival in platform and it can provide seats to let them to sit down in the busy (peak) crowding time. It will make them to feel pleasure, even the MTR ticket fare is not fair and reasonable to charge higher fare to compare other kinds of public transportation tools fares. So the peak waiting time factor can influence the passengers to choose other kind of transportation tools to catch easily. Moreover, MTR's two reference points are the earliest role. Similarly a loss is observed when the MTR platform waiting commuter experiences or actual arrival time which is beyond that the MTR schedule time. Due to that a MTR waiting commuter is as an early side arrival of whose actual arrival time is earlier than whose preferred arrival time.

Reference

Bailey, L., Mokhtarian, P.L. Little, A. (2008). The broader Connection Between Public Transportation, Energy Conservation And Greenhouse Gas Reduction, Report Prepared As Part Of TCRP Project J-11/Tasks Transit Cooperative Research Program, Transportation Research Board Submitted To American Public Transportation Association in http://www.apta.com/research/into/online/

land_use.cfmi, accessed 17 April 2008.

The UK Standing Advisory Committee On Trunk Road Assessment (SACTRA) (1999). Transport And The Economy (Report To UK DETR). Retrieved From: http://webarchive.nationalarchives.gov.uk/ 20050301192906 ; http://dft.gov.uk/stellent/groups/dft-econappr/documents/pdf/dft_econappr_pdf_022512.pdf

Wikipedia Contributors (2008). Arterial Roads In Wikipedia, The Free Encyclopeda, http://en.wikipedia.org/ w/ index.php?title=Arterial_road&oldid=212832640(accessed May30,2008).

What the psychological need differences between rail and bus passengers

● Reasons we need to improve public bus transport tool service quality

The ways that we need to improve public transport, e.g. bus transport service, we try our best to ask these questions: During periods of stress on the bus, like weather conditions or maintenance failure that slows the bus service system? How to improve mass transit on bus service frequency, when looking at ways to improve public bus service transport , riders want frequency? Interestingly, speed is not as much of an issue, if they are waiting downtown in the rain, or on some suburban backstreet, riders want to know that a bus will arrive soon, preferably in less than 15 minutes. Therefore, the wait becomes part of the transportation cycle. Even, if the bus is lightning fast, in the mind of the rider, the trip begins right when they arrive at the bus station, and start waiting for the bus to pick them up.

`

`What does efficient bus ticketing system mean? It is big part of how to improve bus transportation efficiency is improving transit ticketing system, because ticketing systems have to be quick and practical to allow for prompt loading and unloading of passengers. So, inefficient ticketing systems also slow down bus frequency, as drivers need to wait for everyone to tap before they can drive away to the next stop.

How to let passengers feel comfortable? Riders want comfortable buses that can seat as many people as possible. Face-to-face seating is not appealing and being knee-to-knee in a confined space creates awkward moments between strangers. However, comfort also extends beyond the buses' seating arrangements. A smooth riding, quiet bus plays a significant role in reducing the overall stress of a public transit experience. Among the consistent feedback from riders of fuel cell electric buses is a surprised delight about how quiet the buses are when in motion.

On reduce greenhouse gases environment prote3ctoin aspect, exhaust spewing buses are on ongoing concern. One of the significant factors that commuters consider when deciding to take public transit is the environment impact of their alternative transport method. And although a diesel bus packed with 40 people may be less environmentally damaging than 40 separate diesel cars, it will still have negative impacts on both local air quality and the overall climate situation , when given the choice, we've found nearly all riders prefer " zero-emission buses" to conventional diesel buses nowadays.

IN fact, we are always thinking of ways to improve public transportation by dev4eloping new clean fuel technologies. Fuel cell electric buses resolve some of the above issues for both transit bus operators, bus performance is continually being proven and improved over millions of miles of operation in environments ranging from mountain villages to desert communities to busy cities. Hence, the first step to creating better public transit networks is becoming aware of the available options. Many communities are taking measures to improve public transport by implementing innovative sustainable transport solutions that have profound impacts on the live ability of their communities.

So, I shall recommend these ways to improve public transport methods to bus service as below:

Firstly, making interchanging easy for public transport has most efficient public transport service improvement aim at linking areas that are outside a city to the city center., doing this is beneficial in two ways. It helps people who should not at the city center , but needed to pass through because the outlying areas are not connected together to keep off and hence reduce congestion at the center. Also, connecting the outlying areas provide a backup for the public transport system in case of a problem which often happen.

Secondly, minimize the number of stops/ stations, stops and stations improve the efficiency of public transport , but there should be a balance between enabling accessibility with more steps or stations and reducing the costs of operation by increasing transit need of ensure trips are covered in time. Therefore, core should be taken to ensure that stops and stations are located on streets to balance accessibility by commuters on one hand and reduces operating cost on the other hand.

Thirdly, lessen traffic congestion by deploying a number measures. Reducing traffic congestion at city streets could be done, implementing a number of strategies, such as providing lanes dedicated specially for the use of public transport, deploying strict regulations , such as queue bypasses or queue jumps. Another means of reducing traffic congestion is by providing feeds and data from public transport systems, freely to commuters to educate and help them avoid areas of traffic congestion and finally, giving priority to public and trams operating efficiency, increasing the travel time of these engineering mechanism whereby a traffic signal turns green at the light of a public transport at an intersection. All of above these improvements may be future public transport bus passengers service improvement need, if any bus companies hope to increase their bus passengers number absolutely.

● What rail passengers really want rail innovation improvement

Public transport systems, such as rail provides benefits including less traffic congestion, less pollution, safe travels, lower expenditures , less effort and better predictability in comparison to road transport. In fact, bus and train riders experience the most negative emotions in comparison with other transport modes, such as private cars , walking and cycling. Hence, technology has the potential to bring about the changes, needed to increase efficiency of rail transport, e.g. cost-effective ways to improve the quality of public transport and increase ridership may involve comfort and convenience improvement, or technology has the potential to provide more up-to-date information and customized service to train passengers and therefore improve the rail journey experience . On the overall, passenger journey , e.g. the importance of automated traveller information systems, and electronic fare payment collection systems can bring rail passengers look for this information in different interfaces from localized displays installed on platforms to smartphone applications.

Moreover, technology can also improve fare collection and management which of made manually can be prone to error, and time consuming , unified cards, smartphones can make it easier for rail passengers to obtain ticket, with the potential to increase the user satisfaction with the rail system. Because rail passengers demand not only pre-trip information for planning their travels, but also information during journeys, such as punctuality, connections and platform allocation. One extensive review indicates that accurate communication, for example, giving effective way finding information, can optimize passengers' experience with public transport.

Also, technology can facilitate the process of finding free seats on trains, which is a current demand from rail passengers and the cause of stress during the boarding process. IN fact, many rail passengers have specific preferences regarding seats and would appreciate having control of where to sit. So, navigation and way finding information can be delivered directly to passengers to inform where they could stand aiming to board less busy carriages, for example, choosing to travel on a less crowded train, or spreading themselves out on the platform before boarding in respond to crowding information, e.g. smartphones are frequently used by passengers of public transport and can make waiting times seem shorter. Furthermore specific system features designed for train passengers have the potential to improve the journey experience of the travelling public.

What ferry passengers service improvement need

- How can ferry service be improved affordable, reliable, convenient, flexible and clean will get drivers out of their cars ad onto environmentally responsible to passenger ferries?

Ferry transportation provides an environmentally friendly commuting alternative to the congested roadways in many of countries , so ferry transport service needs to meet long term air quality goals, it is critical to move beyond traditional technologies to zero-and near zero emissions technology. Clearly putting a transit system in operation that demonstrates emission control technology and the development of zero-emissions, ferries will help achieve air quality goals to our societies, for example., new shipping rout4es are needed to increase in order to satisfy ferry passengers different rapid ferry journey short distance need, when they need to choose one kind of public transport service either bus or rail or ferry transport service among of them.

None ferry accident occurrence, ferry service needs to let passengers to feel it is the safest sea pubic transit, expanded recreational service is also needs, particularly on weekends when bridge , corridor traffic congestion is becoming an increasing problem. Ferry service needs have uniquely provided flexible, vital transportation supports in response to a natural or man-made disaster that shuts down bridges and roads, fuel –cell technology is needed , that will lead to zero-emissions ferries, e.g. on-board emissions monitoring is far less polluting than previously through, e.g. 149 passenger boats are designed to travel 25 knots or less , and 300-350 passenger vessels designed for speeds up to 30-35 knots.

This emissions standard will perform specifications and the cost of this technology is accounted for in the ferry company vessel capital budget ,e.g. vessel design capabilities to accommodate existing and new docking configurations . This maximizes fast ferry passenger loading, including bicycles, carriages and wheelchairs. Hence, future global ferry service needs have these positive influence to our societies: Need for flexibility, desire to help the environment, need for time saving, which includes the importance of reliability, sensitivity to personal travel experience, such as a need for personal space or quiet feeling ferry seat any time, insensitivity to transport cost, e.g. the ferry ticket price is cheaper than rail or bus fares sensitivity to stress.

However, ferry service is different unlike rail, bus because expanded ferry service can be launched quickly at low initial cost and with great flexibility. Unlike buses, ferries are not hindered by traffic congestion on roads and highways or in tunnels. So, ferry service can be safely expanded to bring new service to new places and add more service to existing routes more easily than bus and rail public transport both, e.g. expanded ferry transport service can operate safety and provide with a robust, flexible and effective emergency response capability if the region is hit with a natural or man-made event that disables roads, other transit, bridges , before any.

Hence, ferry companies need to decide to improve their ferry transport service, they need to answer these questions: Is the new shipping route a good transportation investment? Does the new shipping route have fatal environmental negative impact? Does it offer a transit option that can be initiated in a timely and cost-effective manner? Can it provide ferry transport service that is reliable, safe and fully accessible after the ferry recovery would be unreasonably high charge to ferry selection is decided to implement to increase?

Also, ferry safety is needed to consider because it can influence any ferry passenger choice, when the ferry is moving on the sea, when the passenger is sitting on the boat. The ferry safety issue may include: Ensuring that access to all ferry operational areas, including, machinery spaces, pilothouse and gear lockers, remain locked at all times and accessible only to authorized crew, posting night watch security guards at terminals, conducting diligent onboard inspection for unattended passenger bags, briefcases and packages after each run, before the next boat load is allowed to board, creating coded signals and response to report suspicious activity, requiring positive identification before allowing any contractors, vendors or others access to ferries, providing additional security training to crew, developing a security plan to account for potential threats, outlining preventive measures and detailing an action plan in the event of a threat or actual emergency.

Future Human Transport Need Change

How future our transport need change? What factors influence our future transport need change? In general, these factors may influence our transportation need change. They may include fuel cost, the labor market for commercial drivers, demand for frieight , customer loyalty , vehicle capacity, government regulation, geographical events, the public transport tool reputation to passegners as a merchant. However, the factors that influence the development of transport system in an area? They may include as below:

Environment at the local scale existing hydrographical and geomorphological characteristics are string, factors in transport development, particularly in terms of the technical challenges (bridge, gradients,) they present to construct, other factors may include historical, technological, political and economic factors. All of these factors may influence our future transport system how develops. For raiway development influential factors, they may include: Geograohical factors, e.g. the North Indian plain with its level land, high density of population and rich agriculture presents the most favourable conditions for the development of railways in India. However, the presence of large number of rivers makes it necessary to construct bridges which involve heavy expenditure to Indian Government publich transport expenditure.

How transport has changed from past to present?

There has been a remarkable development in modern transportation. The stream engine and then the stream trains have emerged and spread at this time and in abundance until the discovery of natural gas and oil was an evolution of transportation. Thus, the sedams and vehicles began to run in oil, until present battery changes energy vehicle need, even future non-manual driving artificial intelligent driving vehicle need. These new transport technology may influence our future public transportation from gas energy to battery changed energy, even non-manual driving vehicles need to our daily transport need.

So, our future purpose of public transport need is the unique purpose to oversome space, which is shaped by a variety of human and physical constraints, such as distance, time. These both is our future main public transport need main purpose factors, short distance and reducing journey time, they influence that why we need to choose to catch any kinds of public transportation tool to replace purchase private cars to drive transport tool choice. So, future any kinds of public transport tools, they need to consider above both main factors , how to attract passengers to choose to catch themselves public transport tools choice in this competitive public transport tools market.

On the other hand, the economic importance of transportation development can be defined as improving the welfare of a society, through appropriate social, political and economic conditions , such as US Government spent too much money to assist MTR (MAss transport railway firm) to develop underground thrain transport. Its aim to let many passegner can reduce journey time and reduce distance between destinations, it also hopes US citizen passengers can pay cheap transport fare to buy ticket to catch underground transport train for many families their transport expenditure in social transport welfare view.

However, US Government neds to solve those challenges, before it implements to develop rapid underground railway , e.g. lack of knowledge of geographical fwatures, lack of manpower necessary to operate the rapid underground railway construction work, lack of construction materials within the US itself. For Brazil rail network transportation development example, the factors influence the use of rail network for transportion is highly restricted in Brazil. Thus, the development of roadways and waterways is the main modes of transportation that caould be used in Brazil given its topography and drainage benefit to society . So, brazil can develop rail network for transportation development in success.

So, transportation system is important in the development of any nation, because transportation plays important role in rapid economic growth of a nation. Thrapsortation increases the quality and variety of consumer goods, thereby stimulating the demand and development of trade and economy of the nation. Moreover, transport provides various employment opportunities and boosts up the economy of the country.

Also, any transport tools need to improve themselves transport service in order to attract passengers to choose their public transport service more easily. They may attempt to sign up for an autonomous vehicle pilot program, free phone enquiey concerns whether the passegner can catch which bus bumber to go to the destination, hou much bus fare, how long journey time, when the bus will arrive teh bus stops or leave the bus stop etc. bus service questions, before any one passenger prepares to choose to catch bus (free bus go phone call enquiry), free download a public transport tool transit app. even water taxi tranport tool innovation can replace ferry public transport tool, it can let passengers have more fun an enjoyable catching feeling. So, water taxi tranport tool is one kind of future new transport tool change to replace ferry , it can influence ferry passengers to choose water taxi public transport tool to replace ferry. Although, its fare may be more expsnse to compare ferry, but it can reduce jounrey time and distance between both water stations, when ferry can not arrive the other destinations, but water taxi can arrive any one water station destination. It can bring convenient to future any one ferry passengers. So, water taxi may be developed to some countries, e.g. New Zealand , Auckland city, US , Washington and New York cities they had developed water taxi public transport tools to let ferry passengers have one kind new water public transport choice.

However, instead of new transport innovation improvement to water transport service public transport with input from the public on bus transport service aspect, bus frequency improvement, it means when booking at ways to improve, bus frequency from long times to less times, efficient bus ticketing system, a big part of how to improve tranportation efficiency is improving transit ticketing system.

In fact, my future transport system may still include these five types, modes of transport are: railway, roadways, airways, waterways and piplelines. Also, among different includes of transport, railways are the different modes of transport, railways are the cheapest. Trains cover the distance in less time and comparatively, the fare is also less to other modes of transporation. Therefore, railways is the cheapest mode of transportation to compare ferry, water taxi , sea transport, bus, taxi, road system.

On conclusion, transport price is not the main factor to attract passegners to choose to catch. The importance to have a good public transport system in place. It may be one main factor to help the kind of public transport tool to attract passengers to choose to catch, because a good transport links can widen people's job search area and help them find employment. It can also reduce commuting times and reduce the cost of living, and high skilled workers are more likely to travel across longer distances to work, especially if they are following good job opportunities. So, future any one kind of public transportation tool service provider ought consider how to satisfy working people working time need to shorten journey time to any working places or student learning time need to shorten jounrey times to any schools as well as let they feel comfortable to sit on comfortable chairs or provide free internet service to themselves mobiles , laptops, when they are sitting down or standing up in the kind of public transport . It is the important factor to influence any kind of public transport service in success.

Future Non-Manual driving vehicle How
Influences Public Transport Tool Passenger Need

Nowadays, artifical intelligent (non-manual) driving vehicles are invented, it may be accepted to any countries families to feel comfortable to drive on roads, because any people choose to buy any kinds cars, when any people choose to buy kinds of non-manual (artificial intelligent) vehicles, they do not need to use their hands to drive cars, because artificial intelligent (robotic auto control wheels, it means that robots can help human (drivers) to control wheel to drive to avoid any cars crash occurrence on the roads more easily.

If one day, non-manual driving robotic control whoole vehicles are invented in successful, whether it will persuade many different conuntries families choose to buy non-manual (robotic auto control wheel) vehicles, then it will cause bus, tram, train, underground train, road transport need will be influenced to reduce or even if non-manula boats are invented, whether it will cause ferry sea transport needs will b influenced to reduce. Hence, future non-manual driving vehicles or bats invention whether they will influence public transport tool of road and sea transport passengers number reduces. It is one interesting question. I shall attempt to discuss as below:

In fact, non-manual vehicles are very attraction, to excite any person chooses to buy to drive, because people do not need often touch wheels and touch foots button to control cars to move often forever, when robotic can be invented to help human to control car wheel and foot button, any person only needs to sit on his/her car, then the car can move rapidly, because any drivers is lazy, he/she hopes machine can help her/him to drive car on the road safely. So, he/she can read book or listen music or eatch mobile movie to enjoy his/her entertainment when he/she is sitting on his/her car.He/she will feel more comfortable and enjoyable when robotic can help him/her to drive car. So, robotic (non -manual driving vehicle) can encourage people to choose to buy cars because any drivers won't need to drive cars, robotic can help drivers them to drive on the road easily, when global any one family can own one robotic auto control (non-manual driving) car at least, it may influence these owning non-manula diriving vehicle owners do not feel need to pay any fares to buy road public transport tools of bus ticket, train ticket, underground train ticket , tram ticket to go to anywhere. So, it seems that robotic (non-manual driving) vehicles may influence future any road transport passengers number reduces , because traditional catching any kinds of road public transport tool passengers will be influenced to choose to sit themselves auto (non-manual) driving cars to go to offices to work, parents do not need to follow their sone/daughters to sit on themselves non-manual auto driving cars to go to schools, because their sons/daughters can sit on themselves non-manual driving cars to go to schools more easily. In holidays, they can sit on themselves non-manual driving cars to go to cinemas, music halls, breachs, theaters, shopping centers, gardens different entertainment places to enjoy their any leisure safely because robotic can help them to drive their cars on roads safely.

So, it means that robotic auto control driving cars can influence global every family to feel that they do not need to catch any kinds of public transport tools, e.g. bus, train, tram, taxi underground train to go to anywhere because robotic auto driving cars can help any one, he/she does not know how to drive car to go to anywhere safely. So, future any one won't need to learn driving car skill, when he/she likes to buy one auto driving car. So, in passenger public transport need view, non-manual driving cars will influence them to feel any kinds of road public transport tools can help them to go to anywhere conveniently, because themselves non-manual driving vehicles can help them to drive cars to go to anywhere conveniently. They only need to tell robotic that where they want to go, when they sit on their non-manual driving cars, then robotic knows whether where destination, they want to go, their cars will auto move on the road immediately. It is one exciting and enjoyable ourney when the driver does not need to drive his/her car on the road. So, it seems that robotic (non-manual driving) vehicles invention may bring negative influence to any kinds of public transport tools service needs to passengers , when passengers had owned one non-manual driving car at least.

Why and how non-manual driving car owners need

raise public transport quality on travel time and fare aspects

● How non human driving behavior can be influence by non-manual driving cars

In fact, impact of automated vehicless on travel mode preference, it can bring both trip purposes and distances aim raising need to any kinds of public transport service passegners. Because of technology penetration in the transportation system, the automated vehicle is set to be a future mode of transport, it may bring negative impact to future any kinds of public transport passengers needs, in special on the potential impact of these non-manual driving automated vehicles on travel behaior negative impact to public transport passenger behavior. Automated vehicles will influence future public transportation passengers feel it can bring more short time travel distances and short trip purposes more benefit than any kinds of public transport choices, e.g. bus, taxi, ferry, train, tram, underground tram etc. road and sea public transport tools, e.g. ferry, water taxi. It means that when future any passenger feels above these any one kind of public transport tool needs to spend longer travel time on journey distance and trip to compare future automated vehicles, then they will choose to sit on automated vehicles in preference, due to automated vehicles can help global any one person needs to go to anywhere rapidly.

So, automated vehicles may replace general traditional public transport tools in possible, when they are popular accepted in societies. On the other, instead of shortening journey travel distance time, (travel time) aspect, public transport fare, travel cost will be another influential factor to influence future public transport tool passengers to choose automated vehicles to replace to catch any kinds of public transport tools.

In fact, conventional cars and public transport s are perceivd as being the least attractive alternative in relation to in-vehicle travel time on short and long distance communting trips. So , future automated vehicle drivers (non -human driving) behaviors will be likely changed to prefer this mode for long distance leisure trips rather than short distance commuting trips by automated vehicles.

In fact, advanced technologies have revolutionized many aspects of human life, include the automated vehicle transport system. Also, transport system is one of the essential development aspect to particular , such as non-manual driving automation , vehicle aims to make trips safer, faster , more efficient, automated vehicles passengers and drivers can feel enjoyable to do themselves leisure behavior , e.g. read books, listen, music, listen mobile, watch laptop movies when any one does not need to consider whether their cars are safe to be driven , even any one needs to drive the automated car, because robotic can help them to control how to automatic drive this car on the road safely.

Robotic will bring confidence to let them feel that themselves cars are moving safely on the roads . In recent years, the concept of automated driving has been introduced as on outstanding platform for the next generation of driving systems that is expected to improve safety, traffic flows efficiency, reducing traffic jams occurrence chance, avoiding traffic accidents occurrence chance, e.g. avoid to crash any one person when he/she is walking across road or crach any car is moving on the road easily, capacity, accessibility , and reducing congestion through the application of some technologies , such as vehicle to vehicle and vehicle to infrastructure communication.

So, future automated vechicles can have good driving facility systems to be installed in their cars, in order to raise safety, rapid driving speed level to let any one to feel , when they are sitting in their automated cars, e.g. using cameras, sensors, global positioning system adaptive cruise control, light detection and ranging, and advanced driver assistance system, automated vehicles can steer the vehicle and drive it automatically when passengers delegate control to a computer. Absolutely, ny replacing the driver role with an automated driving system , future one automated vehicle is able to totally free up passengers under automation levels.

So, unless future any kinds of public transport tools may apply automated robotic automated driven system replace the bus driver, taxi driver, train driver, tram driver, underground train driver to raise automated driving system service improvement level to let any one passengers to feel. Otherwise, when automated vehicles are popular to be accepted to buy in any one country in global. Then, global public tansport tool passegners number may be influenced to reduce when global any one family owns at least one automated vehicle at themselves homes .

In other words, automated vehicles can bring thes benefits to let global any one household family feels, future automated vehicles users , they can mostly behave like passengers inside the vehicle, which implies that they will be able to multitask and productive by allocating the travel time to do other activities, e.g. reading, eating, working, drinking, watching movies, listening musics, even sleeping. So, automated vechicles will motivate humans to change non-humanly driven behaviors from conventional humanly driven behavior. This non-humanly driven behavior may be one main factor to influence or encourage future any one kind of public transport passenger won't choose to pay fare to buy ticket to catch any one kind of public transport tool again, because non-manual driven behavior may hel many lazy people do not need to consdierate how to learn to drive cars skills to prepare pass any road test in order to earn the driving licnece to permit to drive cars forever. When automated vehiclesa re popular to be accepted to replace manual-driven cars in societies.

Hence, automated vehicles could potentially change the traditional human driven vehicle market to cause their manual driven cars sale buyers number reduces, when the automated vehicle buyers number increases, also they can chance globa public transport passengers behaviors to reduce to pay fares to catch any kinds of public transport tools when automated vechicles users may sit on themselves automated vehicles to go to anywhere in short time rapidly and safely in any countries.

On conclusion, future global public transport service competition is serious, because instead of global passengers had began to compare whether which kinds of public transport fares are cheaper, more safe, shortening journey time between leaving place and destination, more comfortable feeling, e.g. clean and comfortable chairs , mre free internet service facilities in order to make any one kind of catching public transport tool choice in preference. On the other hand, future automated vehicles number will increase when traditional manual driven car users begin to believe that automated vehicles can bring more safe , more comfortable, more fee- time using, more leisure satisfactory feeling, more than traditional manual driving cars. Then, when global any one household family had made choice to buy at least one automated vehice to replace themselves car(s) at home. When, they are habit to sit in themselves automated vehicles to go to anywhere, however, short or long trip . Consequently, global any one household family won't feel any kinds of public transport tools may bring personal economic saving cost, comfortable, enjoyable, free-time using benefit to compare themselves automated vehicles . It will cause global public transport tools passengers number will reduce , when many different kinds of home automatic vehicles are purchased to replace manual driving cars by global household automated vehicle users. So, in passegner transport tool choice psychological view, automatic vehicles will be possible to replace future public transport service tools. So, any public transport service providers can not neglect how to desing and improve their facilities , charge reasonable transport fare, provide more comfortable, and enjoyable sitting feeling , even applying automatic driving system to replace human drivers in order to attract passegners ' catching need choice more easily.

Artificial Intelligent In Road Transportation Strategy

- How artificial intelligent vehicle may interact intelligent transportation tools

Can artificial intelligence (AI) and machine learning (ML) be used in the search for new " consumption" behavioral type variables that affect consumer individual or transportation service organization individual different transportation tools choices, such as road or sea or sky transportation tools? Can artificial intelligent vehicle may interact intelligent transportation tools market development?

Consumers usually have bargaining and on risk choice when they are already shopping, such as who need to accept to use any (AI) new technological products to replace human traditional behaviors, such as intelligent non-manual driving transportation market, e.g. cars are needed to be driven by human drivers on road, but it has bargaining and on risky choice, when non-manual (AI) vehicle buyers who need to depend on non-manual artificial intelligent (ML) system assists them to drive their cars on the roads.

So, any non-manual driving auto car buyers must need to believe (AI) non-manual driving vehicles (ML) systems can make accurate driving judgement to reduce or avoid any traffic accident occurrences more than human drivers' driving judgement when the (ML) systems are driving their cars on the roads. Then the intelligent vehicle manufacturers will have possible to sell their non-manual driving vehicles success.

This is the first reason or idea influences consumer individual choice to buy any kinds of (AI) non-manual driving vehicles, when consumers believe (ML) systems are more safe and make more accurate judgement to compare human or computer systems, when they are sitting in one non-manual auto driving vehicle on the road.

The another second reason or idea is that some common limits on driving consumer prediction might be understood as the kinds of errors made by poor implementation of machine learning.

Supposing driving consumers believe (AI) machine learning ability is worse to compare to human learning ability. It will also influence driving consumers do not accept to use any (AI) non-manual auto driving vehicles to replace every driver is essential on driving by himself/herself on the road.

The third idea or reason is that it is important to influence driving customers believe how (AI) non-manual auto driving technology is used in them can both overcome and exploit human driving skill and safe limits and raise more auto driving safe judgement to compare human driving safe judgement.

However, how to predict any kinds of (AI) non-manual driving vehicles future consumption effort, due to different kinds of (AI) non-manual driving transportation vehicles which have different unique functions and designs to be used by different kinds of road transportation or driving demand of consumers. For example, lorry drivers need non-manual intelligent system can help them to drive fast, but safe to assist them to transport cargo to arrive destinations from their factories or offices. Otherwise, private car driver expects whose (AI) non-manual driving vehicle can auto drive to send to whom to arrive destination in safe way and non-too fast and non-too slow speed in order to avoid accident occurrences.

So, a different road intelligent consumer demand is to define whose individual driving behavior and driving habit and driving attitude and driving judgement and driving speed demand to decide how to design whose intelligent vehicle to satisfy those driving demand more generally, as simply being open-minded about what variables are likely to influence every consumer economic choice, when who decide either to buy any kinds of (AI) products or not to buy any kinds of (AI) products to replace the different demand of consumers their different (AI) useful demand.

Hence, for these three (AI) products group of stakeholders, such as home (AI) consumer group, firm (AI) consumer group and government (AI) consumer group . These consumer groups may consider whether different kinds of (AI) products can give what is special beneficial interest to them to use. These variables can be measurable properties of choices to influence them to choose to buy any (AI) kinds of (AI) products to use, e.g. psychophysiological, biological, social influences, consumer's wealth, moods and personality, (AI) product price etc. variable factors which will influence them to decide to attempt to buy any kinds of (AI) products to use.

If behavioral economics is as open-mindedness about what variables might predict. Then , (AI) machine learning system is a way to do behavioral economics because it can make use of a wide set of variables and select- which ones predict.

In behavioral economic view point, when general consumer overall demand to the product is much than the other similar (AI) non auto driving vehicle products, such as any kinds of (AI) non-manual auto driving vehicles and any kinds of manual driving vehicles case, then any kinds of (AI) non-manual auto driving vehicles will be more attractive to cause many manual driving vehicle buyers choose to buy (AI) non-manual auto driving vehicles. Hence, it seems if any kinds of (AI) non-manual auto driving vehicle products can make more attractive variable efforts to influence overall driving consumers to feel that they have more needs to drive non-manual auto vehicles to compare more than driving manual driving vehicle.

What is the main variable effort to intelligent vehicles to attract driving consumers to choose to accept to drive them ? However, I believe that (AI) machine learning system is a main factor to raise overall driving consumers' acceptances to drive it to replace manual driving vehicle. If it can persuade or prove (AI) machine learning system ability and judgement effort is more accurate than human or computer learning effort or judgement effort, then it is possible that any kinds of (AI) non-manual driving vehicle products will be accepted to drive on the road in popular.

Machine learning system is able to find prediction value in details of how the bargaining occurs. This discovery is the beginning of the next step for driving consumer individual driving behaviors or driving habits. It raises questions that include: What variables predict to influence driving consumers to change whose driving habits or driving attitudes? How can driving consumer individual emotion, face-to-face talking with whose friends when they are sitting in the non-manual driving vehicle to influence whom driving habit or driving attitude to be changed ? Do driving consumers consciously understand why those habit driving attitudes variables are important when they are sitting in one intelligent vehicle? Can (AI) driving machine learning methods capture the effects of motivated cognition to influence driving consumers decide to buy any kinds of (AI) non-manual auto vehicle products more attractively. So, it seems (AI) driving machine learning method is a main variable factor to influence driving consumers to feel who have more confidence to drive them more than any other kinds of similar manual driving vehicles on the road.

Consequently, (AI) driving machine learning system will be one important psychological method to influence driving consumers to choose to buy (AI) auto driving vehicle products to replace manual driving vehicles. The reason is because human and driving machine learning system both which will have limited variable factors to influence general different countries (AI) driving consumers' need desire to be raised.

- Why can (AI) driving machine learning system main factor influence driving consumer individual desires ?

Driving consumer expectations are hard to measure or

predict driving attitudes and driving behaviors in (AI) non-manual driving vehicles market. Artificial intelligence is another kind of computer science development to apply intelligent vehicle market. Why do driving consumers feel need to buy any kinds of (AI) auto driving vehicles to drive to replace manual driving vehicles on the roads? What are (AI) auto driving features different to manual driving features?

(AI) is the recreation of cognitive functions in computers; it enables machines to perform tasks like humans and perhaps even better than human. In the real world, scientists develop the technological singularity, in which a superintelligence emerges with unfold human consequences.

Professionals in many industries are intensely interested in the specifics of what (AI) can do today, and how can it helps. They are considering the impact of applied (AI), in which computers are used to address a particular problem, extracting and utilizing patterns found in large volumes of data. Of all (AI)'s subfields, machine learning is attracting the most attention. I shall explain why (AI) machine learning system is the main factor to lead consumers feel need to buy any (AI) products to use. Such as below:

For smartphone, fraud detection to medical diagnosis etc. applied (AI) technological products examples. (AI) machine learning systems can help any one of these products to do any exceed general computer learning systems which (AI) learning systems can do any skills to supply (AI) users to use to compare computer learning systems can not do any skills to supply compute users to use. It seems that (AI) machine learning system is the unique feature to attract consumer consideration in technological product market.

An term for different types of learning, and can be

accomplished using different techniques. This has led to a perception that all marketing teams should have (AI) to bring a unified personalized customer experience, when consumers choose to buy any (AI) products to feel what are the different or unique characteristics to compare general computer products. Such as (AI) product has this unique machine learning characteristics, we can predict (AI) and machine learning is connected to influence consumers to feel needs.

Furthermore, over the same time period, and in contrast to predictions for roles in many industries. (AI) won't take the place of marketers and merchandisers themselves although it is already a new value to analytical and strategic marketing skills to persuade consumers to buy any (AI) products. It means different kinds of (AI) products will have different machine learning effort and unique characteristics to attract consumers to choose to buy them to use. Such as, when intelligent vehicles need have unique road driving or sea transportation or flying machine learning system when they are applied on these three kinds of transportation tool aspects. They need have good response safety driving and immediate response learning systems to avoid any boats or air planes or vehicles to crash to them to reduce accident occurrences immediately on any one of either road or sky or sea journey environment.

What is the reason why (AI) driving machine learning system can influence good at making sense to driving consumer desire? Only humans (drivers) , preferably experienced, well informed humans can understand their driving customer needs and decide how to design or reengineer any (AI) intelligent vehicle product functions. (AI) intelligent vehicle can give these professionals the means to do this better to compare manual driving immediate response control function when any vehicles are driving or they will stop immediately to close / near to them in order to reduce crash occurrence on the road, and then maximize relevance through real-time customization of the non-manual auto vehicle driving user experience.

For example, as ever, senior decision makers need to be informed, decisive and results-oriented or risk losing out. Harvard Business Review indicated : Over the next decade, (AI) won't replace managers, but managers who use (AI) will replace those who don't. Such as intelligent vehicle won't replace drivers, but drivers who use intelligent vehicles will replace those who can not control how to drive their vehicles in the most safe way. So, (AI) driving machine learning system will have possible to do any drivers' (human's) driving judgement, driving analytical mind and driving effort to be more accurate than manual driving skills. Such as how to control to drive the intelligent vehicle in the most safe way. It is general manual driving skill can not achieve to drive in the safe way.

For another (AI) digital commerce example, (AI) and machine learning are the most exciting developments in marketing and merchandising to be applied to digital commerce, such as making better decisions through trend and cluster analysis, deploying product and content in mutually reinforcing combinations, increasing customer engagement and satisfaction in real time.

Hence, the key attraction in digital commerce circles is that machine learning is designed to be self-optimizing. Optimizing for revenue example will surface are increasingly profitably selection of products (within the brand parameters selected).

When to apply (AI) capabilities and what value (AI) is delivering for customer and company like. Unlike any technology before it, (AI) is analytical and predictive capabilities offers the prospect for each and every individual. It can maximize real time and engagement. Effective tailored (AI) technology, such as digital experience cloud technology is available now. And once integrated, (AI) starts learning and delivering incremental value from day one. So (AI) could transform the digital experience to any business organizations.

Hence, (AI) driving machine learning system can be applied to road driving skill aspect. When intelligent vehicles are invented to own the most safe driving judgement skill and they can know when either they may auto drive fast speed, when they are feeling to know when there are not many vehicles are moving close/near to them or when they need auto drive slow speed, when they are feeling to know when there are many vehicles are moving close/ near to them. Then driving consumers will have more confidence to choose to buy any kinds of intelligent vehicles to replace manual driving vehicles to drive on the roads.

- Non-manual driving transportation tool market development

If Non-manual driving vehicle manufacturers expect their (AI) automatic vehicles can attract drivers to buy. I feel them to need to consider how (AI) driving machine learning system can achieve these requirements in order to satisfy manual driving vehicle drivers‘ requirement to change their traditional driving habit to choose non-manual driving needs. It means (AI) driving machine learning systems can help them to drive vehicles to replace manual driving vehicles on the road. This is the main factor to influence car buyers choose to buy intelligence driving vehicles replace to manual driving vehicles. I believe (AI) non-manual driving vehicle machine learning systems, need to be designed as below:

(1) Improving driving safety by preventing accidents from happening.
Every year, drivers are facing a large number of casualties, due to traffic accidents. The amount of killed and injured road traffic related accidents is increasing every year. The real cost of an accident can go well beyond the limits of immediate material destruction, and is impossible to evaluate.
Hence, researchers and car manufacturers are looking for solutions in order to reduce the amount of accidents. They already developed a considerable set of technologies in order to decrease the amount of casualties. Most of them (like airbags, seat-belts, anti-lock systems, shock absorbing car bodies) are efficient in decreasing the impact of an accident, and in protecting the passengers of the cars. The technologies already saved a lot of lives, but they are rarely able to avoid accidents because they do not anticipate them. Moreover, if they are protecting in many cases, the passengers of the car, they do not prevent most traffic participants, like pedestrians on bicyclists from getting injured. it causes (AI) non-manual automatic car manufacturers need to consider how to design machine learning safety system is to prevent accident from happening instead of just reducing their impact.
This can only be possible using intelligent systems that can observe the driving environment, reason and decide if there is a danger, determine how to avoid it and act if necessary

(2) Reducing energy consumption by optimizing the driving.

Nowadays, global air pollution is serious. (AI) non-manual driving car manufacturers need to concern how to design (AI) machine learning system can reduce degree of air pollution to be the most minimum level to compare to traditional manual driving vehicles.
The reduction of energy consumption if certainly one of the main challenges. Transportation is one of the major factors in fossil energy consumption, and it is also responsible for a large amount of CO2 pollution. It is difficult to ask individuals to voluntarily limit the use of their vehicle of they do not have a strong incentive to do so. Specially in regions where vehicles are needed to drive to go to work every day. It stands to reason that if it is difficult to decrease the amount of vehicles, part of the solution is to make them more energy efficient.
Hence, non-manual driving car manufacturers need to design how to improve engines, which are more optimized and need less fuel to operate, and hybrid and electric cars have been developed and are continuously being improved. But we can go beyond these solutions that do not take into account the environment in which a vehicle is driving. A growing number of scientific contributions presented intelligent systems used in order to improve energy efficiency and reduce fuel consumption, based on the optimization of the way (AI) non-manual driving (AI) vehicles are performing. Such as recharge batteries and electric engine will be predicted the popular fuel in order to limit fuel consumption to future (AI) non-manual driving vehicles. They can reduce air pollution, consume less fuel for (AI) non-manual driving vehicles.

(3) Improving comfort by anticipating (AI) non- manual driving vehicle drivers.

Finally, another application for intelligent vehicle is the

improvement of driving comfort. Car industry is very competitive market. Many potentials (AI) intelligent vehicle customers need to enjoy to sit more comfortable intelligent vehicles, who will be attracted by (AI) comfortable systems improving when driving, so part of the research in intelligent systems from cars focuses on how to improve the driving experience, i.e. make it easier and more enjoyable, more comfortable to compare to traditional manual driving vehicles.

As an example, lane keeping assistant systems are technologies that actively keep the vehicle in the lane in highways of the driven drifts out of it. Automatic speed regulation keeps the car at a certain speed without requiring to touch the gas pedal. This can be really interesting for, e.g. (AI) non-manual driving truck drivers that spend a lot of time on highways. But these technologies have a limitation in the case of automatic speed regulation, this technology can not copy of a vehicle ahead drives slower than the desired speed, or if another vehicle cuts into the lane.

This case requires the driver to have a constant focus on the road. In order to achieve more comfort, it is better of the system can adapt to changes in its dynamic environment: let the (AI) intelligent vehicle adapt to the speed of the man-manual vehicle, or autonomously change lane when requires. Again, this requires knowledge about the environment, detection capabilities, reasoning and action planning. Intelligent systems can be used in order to create more attractive and more comfortable and more safe, less energy consumption and less fuel expenditure by intelligent vehicles.

HOW DESIGNING UNDERGROUND MASS TRANSIT

RAILWAY TO BRING PASSENGERS

● Designing transportation system advantages

Nowadays, transportation and economic development have close relationship. Economic development stimulates transportation demand by increasing the numbers of workers commuting to and from work, customers traveling to and from services areas, and products being moving by lorries on the roads between products and customers. According to Bailey, Mokhtarian and Little (2008) indicated "transportation route is past of distinct development pattern or road network and mostly described by regular street patterns as an important factor of human existence, development and civilization. The route network combined with increased road transportation investment result in changed levels of conveniently reflected through cost benefit analysis, savings in travel time, and other benefits. " These benefits are noticeable in increased catchment areas for services and facilities , shops, schools, offices, banks and leisure activities.

What are the crisis of neglection to care transporation system ? Why do any countries need to design road transportation system? For example, the Japan country lacks design road trsnaportation system effectively. So, the crisis of road traffic fatalities will raise and the econominc influence will be changed. The crisis indicates more than 7,000 people die annually as a result of motor vehicle crashes in Japan. Driving when under the influence of alcohol is the leading cause of motor vehicle crash fatalities in both developed and developing countries. So, alcohol is the most serious factor to raise personal risk when drivers are driving in Japan. However, a number of studies have shown that deterring drink driving is an important way to cause fatalities. There is a demonstrative need for social change in Japan.

Japan has recently strengthened its already strict laws in order to reduce the number of alcohol related road fatalities. Those deforms lowered the legal blood alochol contant limit increased, the penalties for offenders. The Japan road traffic legal needs. Any driving a motor with a alcohol limit of 0.03 or higher Japan's maximum sentence is up to 3 years imprisonment or a fine not exceeding 500,000 yen dollars. Is law impact to reduce drinking alcohol to drive in Japan? What are economic influence of the crisis of road traffic fatalities in Japan?

The rational choice theory of offending suggests that offenders are active decision makers who influence a large number of variables into decision whether or not to commit an offence. On the cost-benefit analysis, it is the punishment a possible jail, large fines worth is the reward the convenience of driving home without the expause of a taxi and innovenience to the alcohol drivers in Japan. Instead of law reforms when it detects alcohol in the air exhaled from the alcohol and other offenders and it educates children about the dangers of drinking and it also explains why alcohol driving can also threaten drivers' life when who are drinking alcohol and driving behaviour in the same time in Japan.

On the economic influence hand, implementation of the policy deregulating alcohol sales and alcohol production did not appear to increase traffic fatalities among adult or teenage males or females in Japan. We found that male adult fatalities demonstrated a statistically significant decline following enactment of the deregulation policy in 1994 year. So, Japan implement law to threaten alcohol drinking behaviour is useful. It can influence the alcohol availability and consumption, alcohol production and sales, the 24 hours operated convenience stores or liquor discount stores incomes to be reduced. Even, Japan overall GDP is also reduced from the deduction of liquor alcohol production and sale, also the occurrence of traffic accident fatalities chances will be also reduced.

The Japanese economy has entered a rapid process of liberalization since the mid-1990 year. Many sectors previously under direct government control are now regulated by the competitive market place. The Japanese alcohol beverage market has changed. The entry of cheaper import alcohol products resulted in a encouragement of alcohol consumption to Japan drinking drivers and an raising of increasing of more import alcohol products supply to Japan. Although, it is beneficial to Japan GDP growth. But it also raise the occurrence of chance to traffic accidents rate to cause alcohol drinkers to be death or hurt when who choose drinking alcohol to drive at the same time in Japan. So, alcohol import can bring more consumption, but it can also raise many traffic accidents occurrence in Japan in the same time.

In conclusion, alcohol is not good for health to drink when the consumer often buys alcohol at drink habitually. So, if many Japanese, including the alcohol driving consumers and the alcohol non drinking consumers both who often buy different countries alcohol to drink daily. It will cause their bodies to be unhealth for long term in Japan. It is possible to increase Japan's government's medical expenses to assist the low income or poor people in the future. So, although alcohol import can raise Japan GDP growth in the short term, but it also raise Japan government's medical expenditure to the low income or poor Japanese long term in the future, So it's economic benefit will not good in the future if Japan still import much alcohol to sell in its country.

Many commercial users depend on road transport facilities, with movement of products and services from place to place on the roads, aspect of global and urban economic survival. Hence, developments of various transportation modes have become important to physical and economic developments. For example, urban locations with such relative advantages are found where different transport routes with high degree of connectivity, within the intra and inter urban road networks. On similarly, commercial activities like banking, retail/wholesale businesses and professional services can take advantage of nearness to concentration of activities attracted consumers service providers. This partly caused increase in demand for commercial space and its effects on commercial property values along commercial roads can be rose. However, some countries' roads need to provide pedestrian movements more than the businesses activities, e.g. shorten the time of lorries parking on the road to let pedestrian movements on the narrow road. If the country government did not consider the roads need to let more pedestrian movements or shorten the time of lorries parking on the road. It will cause traffic jam or traffic density of the individual roads. Hence, governments need to concern the locations of commercial property buildings and the relationship between the explanatory variables of the design road networks.

What are construction of roads design networks benefits? In fact, construction of roads increased substantially with the opening up of residential environments that also is getting much benefits from increasing demand for spaces in commercial properties. Many private companies, retail stores, commercial banks aggregate in the main roads of cities, which get advantage of opportunities afforded by locations near central of cities to attract many pedestrians concerning their businesses existence. This led to high concentration of vehicular and pedestrian movements. Specially along the access main roads in the central of cities. The main roads exhibits linkages to form networks of minor routes along which commercial properties locate. If commercial users are displaced residential users, causing sites to be at the highest and best uses with increases in the values of commercial properties. However, it seems road network development is affected by the compact nature of various routes that sometimes causes volume of traffic jam. Thus, demand for transport can't be treated solely as a derived demand road. Improved main and minor roads access an city or rural areas is a necessary (but not sufficient). Precondition for increased productivity, the UK Standing Advisory committee On Trunk Road Assessment (SACTRA, 1999) noted "various ways in which transport can affect economic growth, for example benefits include through reorganization and rationalization of production, distribution and land use: reducing labor costs by expanding catchment areas etc."

What is land use and road transport design system relationship? Land use refers to the whole range of human activity and of the built environment, and to some aspects of the natural environment. This is a way relationship between land use and road transport. Governments need to design how to use land and how to design road transportation systems. e.g. where are built the main roads and/or where are built the minor roads are the most suitable locations in the cities or rural areas ? If the main roads is located in the not suitable locations at the centers of the cities or rural, it will case the increasing traffic volumes and levels of congestion, including air pollution, noise, ground water pollution from run-off , loss of soil functions and loss of bio-diversity to natural environment. By influencing the spatial structure of locations in the urban environment, so land use planning can help to mitigate any negative effects resulting from land use changes.

Modelling and land use transportation interactions has become an important aspect of road design transport planning. On the one side, for example, design roads in urban centers, it can increase land use and it can also reduce employees or students catching buses or driving cars' time spending to go to workplaces or schools users. Hence, the land use and roads designing transportation can give benefits to residents and employment people to reduce time to wait buses or taxies etc. public transportations to go to workplaces or schools or shopping centers etc. anywhere. It seems to assist bus companies or taxi drivers to earn more income, On the other side, designing urban transport systems is also important . Increased densities mean more destinations become within convenient walking and cycling distances and consequently the use of these modes tends to be higher. Also in dese cities public transport systems are able to offer higher levels of service and operate more economically, when the provision of sufficient road space to meet potential demand becomes impractical. It aims to reduce the danger of driving or walking in urban areas. The transport modes (that is walking, cycling, public transport) and the extent of car dependence is less, due to driving users dependency is less on rural roads. Hence, building main roads can concentrate on designing convenience to pedestrian walking to close to their houses on the streets. However, poor transport design and land use can cause to spend too expenditure not only transport costs on governments and transport users both and also the costs of providing other services. These include the usual utilities and also education and health services as well as negative externalities , such as greenhouse gas emissions. Most such studies concluded that there are significant financial and economics cost advantage of inner city redevelopment compared with fringe development.

However, such policies won't necessarily be successfully, in particular because of the two ways road problem, they may result in additional private investments and employment opportunities flowing into the region, buy may equally result in population and employment opportunities flowing out of the target region because of the improved access to other centers. Hence governments need to analyze how to arrange the land use to assist the property developers to choose where are the suitable locations to build offices or factories or shopping centers or houses at capital or urban cities to adapt to whose the growth of living population. For example, to judge where the land use whether where main roads or junior roads are built where are the suitable locations to satisfy the lorry drivers to park their lorries are the safe locations ; to design the minor roads to let the pedestrians to feel no danger to walk on the streets when the cars are driven to near to the streets on the minor roads. Thus, the factor of choosing where the land use to design the main or minor roads areas, sizes and lengths and of the minor or major roads can influence the drivers and pedestrians feel safe or dangerous when who are driving whose cars on the roads or who are walking on the streets to arrive the offices, schools, cinemas, church, houses etc. destination.

Designing road transportation networks how to assist economic growth ? I feel it is not all transport investments will be equally effective in enhancing economic growth. Designing road transport investment is a necessary, but on its own not sufficient requirement to earn significant economic growth at either a national or regional level. There are conditions under three categories: economic conditions, investment conditions and political conditions. In fact, although in some circumstances, transport investment may be a necessary condition for enhancing economic growth, it is rarely on its own a sufficient condition. Other factors including the broader policy environment, need to be present if the investment is going to be successful in addressing regional economic objectives. My some suggestions the following key aspects as being most relevant including:

a. Scale economies for example, where these dominate, lower transportation costs through improved accessibility may encourage increased concentration of firms in core regions, until the point that diseconomies set in.

b. Size of the local market.

c. Local land and labor conditions.

d. The nature and scale of transport improvements.

e. The nature of backward and forward linkages
in the country 's local economy.

In any countries, road transportation improvements don't guarantee increased economic development. To increase economic development, an improvement needs to assist any lorry drivers to drive in short trips to reduce transportation costs and shorten time driving on the road or to make transportation more reliable, e.g. reducing the numbers of traffic jams on any roads. A proper economic climate must also exist as well as other support services.

With these factors to influence transportation improvements can become catalysts for economic expansion. However, road transportation improvement that intends to induce job creation, when employers need many lorry drivers to help them to transport products and to move products on the roads often. So, the employers need to employ many transportation workers and lorry drivers to help who to transport their products to send to clients, due to the transportation time is shorten and work efficiency is rasied, so the transportation times are also increasing every day when the road transportation roles are improved. On the other side, improving transportation can raise productivity when many customers need to buy many products and the lorry drivers may drive whose lorries to transport many products between factory and office or between factory to the client's home or between the shop and the client's on the road in the short time fast.

I recommend one model links in an overall road transportation network includes these four modes.

I. Maximizing use of the existing road highway system.

II. Extending or improving the multi-lane divides system local roads and connectors.

III. Continually improving the entire road highway network in response to business activities demand.

The improvement of modern road transportation successful factors include:

- How to improve the highway network

modernization includes obsolete interchanges and other segments of the road, transport network of new designs to improve the life and service of pedestrian walking streets, rebuilding certain in main or minor roads. To the extent that labor markets operate more efficiently and more jobs are created to raise economic expansion if our governments can improve road transportation system to design to satisfy business users demand when lorry drivers need to move or transport whose products on the streets, but who will not influence pedestrian are walking on the streets. Hence, excellent transportation design network can subsequent plan efforts, it can also rise economic efficiency, community and social effects, it can also encourage transportation users to attempt to drive lorries to transport products a lot of times in one day fast and who can also avoid traffic jams occurrence on the road easily. On the one side, economic development is a concept referring to the material aspects of community welfare. There are numerous factors need of development: growth in income and wealth, equitable distribution of income, decreased infant mortality rates, increased literacy rates. On the other side, economic growth means which is sustainable increase in community income and /or wealth. (wealth is the net of resources that generate income). It seems the link between transportation facilities and economic growth has close relationship. Good transportation facilities support economic growth by lowing the transportation costs of users of the transportation network, such as roads. Direct users benefits are reductions in travel, times and fuel consumption, increased reliability and increased safety in the movement of people and products, users' transportation costs are reduced, resources are used for other purpose.

The relationship between transport and economic development occur in two directions, in the sense that (i) land use and economic development are major drivers' of demand for transport (in terms of quantity , type, location and mode); and (ii) transportation investments and other initiatives (such as regulations, pricing) can influence levels, patterns and locations of economic development.

The principal role of road transportation is to provide access between spatially separated locations for the business and household sectors, for both commodity (lands transportation) and person movements. For the business sector, this involves connections businesses and their input sources between business factories and other business shops and between business and their markets. For the households sector, it provides people with access to workplaces and education facilities, shops and social recreation, community and medical facilities etc. on the roads. I feel different countries' road transportation system can be self funded in the sense that the majority of the costs of transportation system investment operation and maintenance are either paid directly by users (for example, through car operating costs) are funded initially by governments and recovered from transport users (for example, through petrol duties and road user charges). Governments' road transportation system and their use also give rise to some external costs(externalities). These include global environmental impacts (greenhouse gas emissions) and local environmental and health impacts (for example, noise partial pollution and road accident costs). The direct effects of transportation investments are to reduce road transportation time and costs through reducing travel time, decreasing the operating costs of transportation and enhancing access to destinations within the road network. A good road transportation network also needs to reduce any economic disbenefits, for example where projects reduce congestion or the risk of injury. These incremental benefits of transportation investments may be measured through commercial cost benefit analysis. Other indirect consequences of road transportation network should also be considered when evaluating effects on productivity and the spatial pattern of economic development. Good road transportation design network benefits can include lower costs and enhanced accessibility, due to better transportation links and services expand markets for individual transportation using business and improved access to input.

The economic contribution of road transportation policy can be assessed from various perspectives. These include:

- Effects on aggregate economic welfare (e.g. the sum of consumer and which is the times of cost benefit analysis, as linking to transportation productivity effect.
- Micro economic, for example, enterprise or household level productivity effects.
- Macro economics, for example, contributions to GDP investment or employment and the spatial patterns of economic activity.

One key characteristics of road transportation is split between infrastructure and operations. Infrastructure refers to the right of way on which vehicles operate, which may include ancillary facilities to ensure efficient and effective operations (for example, traffic signals, railway stations). In developed countries, are in most transportation is operated by the private cars, road trucks, the majority of bus and coach services. In long term , overall purpose, to ensure transportation system helps to develop that maximizes the economic and social benefits and minimizes harm. Hence, governments need to concern who are their main target users to use every road. Such as the road is used to near to park and leisure, or local and national economic conditions, keep clean natural environment etc. facilities to provide different benefits to different target users to enjoy to use. It seems that good transportation networks designing can influence economic activities, shopping convenience or business convenience etc. activities to cause whether the country's economic behavior to achieve close relationship successfully. Possible relationship between road networks, location attribute, demand and supply and accessibility and commercial property values of these factors which will influence different countries' concerning to choose where to build main roads and sub minor roads in different cities and rural locations. However, I shall suppose hypotheses how governments to find the most suitable places to build main roads and sub minor roads to whose cities and rural. There is no significant relationship between commercial property values and individual contributions of explanatory variables to variability in commercial property values in whose countries.

In conclusion, I suggest methods how to design suitable transportation networks to governments to build, such as it is essential to establish a technique that may be useful for determining relative accessibility of locations in the network of main roads and sub minor roads. Even, when relative advantages are determined, there is need to develop models that will be useful for predicting commercial properly values. The model may become tool for professional estate surveyors and values to change their practice of using intuition to determine relative access of locations in a road network. Similarly, there is the need to predict the supply of, demand for, and fair market values of commercial properties by developers. Hence if the cities or rural locations can attract many businesses to build commercial properties, governments can build the main roads in the locations. Otherwise, if the cities or rural locations can not attract many businesses to build commercial properties, governments can build the sub minor roads in these locations. Hence, the main roads must have high transportation valuation to let big lorries to drive and park in these main roads easily and conveniently. It seems capital cities may not influence to build the main road factors. Natural environment, commercial properties values, the lands areas size and shape and pedestrian walking numbers on the streets and lorries available numbers on the areas will be other factors to influence where to build main roads in any cities or rural in the country.

In road concept, the route network consists of primary and secondary roads, known as main roads and minor roads respectively. Main roads are usually moderate or high capacity roads that are below highway level of service, carrying large volumes of traffic between areas in urban centers and designed for traffic between neighbors. They have intersections with collector and local streets and commercial areas, such as shopping centers, petrol stations and other businesses are located along such roads. In additions, main roads link up to expressways and freeways with inter-changes in cities or rural. Road network constitutes an important element in urban development , due to urban areas have many farms, gardens, forests , so roads and building needed to provide accessibility required by different land uses and the proper functioning of such urban areas depends an efficient transport network existence. In computing des, the network indicator are used to partition road network into different parts in reasonable way. The results in number of connection to describe density differences in road networks. The parameter records how many roads connect to each road in a network.

For two roads with the same length, the ones in the dense area will connect to more roads than that in a sparse area and the connection differences will indicate the density differences to some extent, so road density can also be calculated as the total length of all known roads divided by the total land area in a road divided by the total land area in a road network. Hence, governments need to consider road length to decide how to build main or minor roads to design its transportation systems for businesses activities , such as driving lorries and parking lorries and products are been moving on the streets from roads easily and conveniently. As Wikipedia Contributors (2008) indicate that "transport networks are spatial structures designed to channel flows from the points of demand to points of supply and to link the points together in a transportation system. They are useful for transport network analysis to determine the flow of people, products, services and vehicles." Hence, governments need to research whether where the shopping centers, cinemas, houses, hospitals, schools, offices, factories etc. are located, then, which need to follow these location datas to predict the cars, lorries, taxies, buses etc. of the demand numbers of transportation users to design the lengths, width and distances and the construction of main and minor roads locations and their supply numbers in different capital cities or country roads. It aims to reduce traffic jams and shorten time and air pollution as well as increasing the available spaces to let the lorry drivers to move their logistc on the road easily and reducing the accidents occurrence when the pedestrians are walking on the streets. If the vehicles can be moved on the roads easily. It will also increase time efficiency and productivity to any businessmen. Hence, how to design of the main roads and/ or minor roads in any capital or country cities. It will influence any country's economic growth long time in the future.

- Underground train transportation needs to know passenger behaviour reasons

Understanding individual passenger behaviour is essential for the design MTR transportation, because who can choose to catch bus, taxi, tram, train ferry etc. different kinds of public transportation tools. Individual traveler who decides to catch which kinds of public transportation tools, it depends on whether the public transportation tool can provide real time travel information, liking link travel time schedule. So, MTR underground train needs to understand where it has terminal to give convenience to the local living areas of time travelers to choose to catch MTR easily. Although, MTR ticket fare is one factor to influence any passengers choice. But, those other factors can also influence them to choice. e.g. MTR any terminal location of convenience, short time travelling, none crowding in busy (peak) time, MTR platform waiting arrival time, none sudden MTR engineering machines broken accident events occurrence frequently etc. different factors, any one of these factors which can influence passengers who choose to catch MTR or other kinds of transportation tools.

Why route choice can influence passenger behavioural choice ? Usually, the busy time passengers will regard the route choice as a coordination problem to influence them to choose to catch which kinds of transportation tools. The route choice is as an opportunity costs to influence any busy time passengers to decide to choose to catch which kind of transportation tool which is the best right choice in the right time among of them. In the short time, for example, it seems any busy time passengers will choose to catch bus to substitute MTR underground train transportation tool, due to who feels the bus can arrive any destinations to compare other kinds of transportation tools in the most short time. However even if the MTR can either charge cheaper ticket fare to sell full day or charge discount ticket fare to sell in the busy (peak) time to compare to bus fare. It is possible that the busy time passengers will still choose to catch bus, if between the bus terminal and the another bus terminal that distance is the shorter time route to spend time to arrive destination to compare between the MTR terminal to the another MTR terminal arrival time . Also, although the busy time passengers will feel to enounter traffic jam to influence sitting or waiting bus time to be longer time in possible and who also feel MTR can avoid traffic jam problem. However, usually any busy (peak) time passengers will feel the chance of traffic jam occurrence will be less. So, the short bus route choice is more potential factor to influence the busy (peak) time passengers still to choose bus to catch.

However, if anyone wants to investigate results of day-to-day route choice which can be transferred to more realistic environment. It is necessary to explore individual behaviour in an interactive experimental set up to ensure busy (peak) time passenger transportation behavioural choice. For example, a passenger has a choice between a main road (M) and a side road (S) for travelling from (A) to (B). (M) is faster if (M) and (S) are chose by the same number of passengers. So, this method can be researched whether MTR terminal station is located at the main road (M) or the side road (S) where is more suitable to accept to passengers generally.

Why trip time reliability and crowding factors can

influence MTR passenger choice? Other problem is MTR busy (peak) time's crowding in public transportation occurrence of MTR underground train transportation tool is becoming a growth to concern as MTR demand growth at a busy (peak) time. To capture the MTR passengers benefits with reduced crowding from improved MTR public transport service and image. It is necessary a identify the relevant dimensions of crowding that are meaningful measures of what crowding means to MTR passengers. Two main influences on MTR model choice that are growing in relevance are trip time reliability and crowding. It represents a benefit-cost framework. In fact, MTR passengers can be willing to pay more expensive ticket fare, it MTR can avoid crowding and short and the accurate arrival trip time between terminals is reliable to occur. How to measure of MTR crowding, e.g. weighting the gap between the busy time, the standard (i.e. objective) and the perceived (i.e. subjective) metrics. We are not in a position to definitely map the two dimensions, which is a crucial requirement for translating objective improvements into equivalent subjective gains that then can be applied, willingness to pay estimates MTR ticket fares to obtain the additional MTR passenger benefits of MTR public transportation investment to any terminal stations. Because MTR crowding has a negative impact on passengers in terms of psychological on emotional distress. MTR passengers are willing to stand for up to 20 minutes of the service is fast and reliable. However crowding outweighed these benefits from a MTR passenger's perpective, experienced crowding leads a increased dissatisfaction. e.g. stress and less privacy during who needs to stand up in MTR. Due to there are no enough places to supply to them to stand up in MTR. If the MTR trip time was longer time between the passenger's terminals, who will feel more dissatisfaction and it will cause who feels whether who ought need to choose to catch other transportation tools to substitute MTR next time. e.g. bus, train, tram, ferry, taxi etc. So, from an operator's perspective, the MTR service frequency or MTR size is significantly influenced by the level of ridership, which sends a signal to respond if the monitored crowding level exceeds the benchmark standard in the busy time. e.g. in the morning time or at the night time, the students or employment people who need to go to schools or offices (working places). The locations of different places between MTR terminals and crowding are regarded as a key service attribute for MTR pubic transportation along with other factors, such as travelling time and reliability, e.g. service quality, none engineering machines are broken to cause MTR stops suddenly.

Given the increasing importance of crowding on both the disutility to existing MTR public transportation users and the influence to it. MTR passenger can choose to use either the MTR public public transportation or other public transportation. It is timely to review the MTR current measures of crowding defined by transportation authorities. MTR operators ought evaluate whether they apporpriately reflect MTR each traveler experiences and perceptions of crowding in busy (peak) time. I suggest that MTR needs to buy other underground trains to supply to the busy (peak) time passengers to let them have enough seats to sit down, so who do not need to stand up in any MTR underground trains when they catch MTR underground trains in busy time. It aims to let who are willingness to pay the estimation of reasonable ticket fares to compare the other kinds of transportation tools in the busy (peak) time.

What is the crowding difference between train and MTR underground train? In fact, crowding won't be happened to brother these transportation tools easily in the busy time and non busy time both. e.g. bus, taxi, train, tram, ferry. Because passengers can not choose to stand up in these transportation tools easily, due to these transportation tools have no enough areas (spaces) to let them to stand up easily . So, the crowding will be avoided to occur in these tranportation tools usually. Otherwise, MTR will have many passengers who can choose to stand up because MTR design of length is very long and it has enough areas (places) to let passengers to choose to stand up, even there have none any seats are provided to let them to sit down. So, MTR passengers will feel more dissatisfaction and crowding easily, especial in any peak (busy) time every day.

Comparing to bus, much more diverse crowding measures are defined in the passenger rail industry. For passenger, different specifications for measuring crowding are found across countries and even within a country. For example, rail crowding measures in the UK, the passengers in excess of capacity is crowding measure that applies to all London and South east operators weekday train services at a London terminus during the morning peak from 0700 to 09: 59 , and those departing during the afternoon peak from 16:00 to 18:59 (office of rail regulation 2011 year). The overall PIXC figure is considered the planned standard class capacity of each train service as well as the actual number of standard class passengers on the service at the critical point. i.e. the location on a trains of standard class passengers that surpass the planned capacity as the difference between the number of actual passengers and the capacity of the train divided by the number of passenger is within the capacity . So, it seems train and MTR underground public transportaton tools had been encountering the crowding problems in peak time, the difference in train passengers need to wait next train or more train arrival is who doesn't plan to enter the train, when who discovers the current train has no seats to provide to them to sit down in whose trip. Otherwise, MTR passengers can choose either to stand up within the large areas (places) if who discovered there are no any seats to provide to them to sit down or who can wait the next MTR arrival in order to who can sit down. It seems MTR transportation tool crowding environment includes in waiting platform and inside of the MTR underground train. Otherwise, train transportation tool crowding environment only includes the waiting platform and the passengers will not have crowding feeling inside of the train, due to none of passengers choose to stand up inside any trains because any train inside has no enough places to let them to stand up.

How MTR can attract many passengers. On the commuter departure time choice of any reference point researching hand, the departure time decisions of communters are of fundamental importance of peak period MTR traffic congestion. However, whether on the demand side, MTR underground train congestion relief measures, such as MTR ticket fare to every terminal station needs to be charged cheaper fare or discount fare in the peak (busy) time every day. To aim to attract many passengers to choose to catch MTR Underground train public transportation tools, substitute to choose other public transportation tools in the peak time.

Over the past decades, there have been very active research

efforts in the departure time problem, both in econometric modeling and dynamic user equilibrium fields. Although, these works provide valuable insights into dynamic commuter decision making, they do not identify the commuters' response to gains and losses related to whole actual arrival time to reference points who may have relative. The appliability of the reference point hypothesis of prospect theory to the commuter's departure time decision making to obtain a better understanding of how departure time choice in MTR platform during their waiting underground train arrival time. However, every MTR underground train actual arrival time and deviation variables related to reference points (gains and losses) are the key factors in the departure time choice model. How the MTR underground train of every communter's daily departure time decision can be modelled when the reference point hypothesis of prospect theory. The MTR underground train's schedule delay is defined as the difference between the preferred arrival time (PAT) and the actual arrival time (AT) for a given MTR communter. In a daily MTR commute, a commuter in the indifference band actual arrival time is an essential feature of MTR schedule study. Two reference points are the earliest acceptable arrival time and the work starting time for a given MTR platform waiting passengers. In psychological view point, prospect theory proposes that the displeasure of a loss is perceived or greater than the pleasure of a gain of the same attitude and therefore, the value function is stronger for losses than gains.

To conclude, it seems that if MTR waiting passengers need not spend long time to wait underground train arrival in platform and it can provide seats to let them to sit down in the busy (peak) crowding time. It will make them to feel pleasure, even the MTR ticket fare is not fair and reasonable to charge higher fare to compare other kinds of public transportation tools fares. So the peak waiting time factor can influence the passengers to choose other kind of transportation tools to catch easily. Moreover, MTR's two reference points are the earliest role. Similarly a loss is observed when the MTR platform waiting commuter experiences or actual arrival time which is beyond that the MTR schedule time. Due to that a MTR waiting commuter is as an early side arrival of whose actual arrival time is earlier than whose preferred arrival time.

Reference

Bailey, L., Mokhtarian, P.L. Little, A. (2008). The broader Connection Between Public Transportation, Energy Conservation And Greenhouse Gas Reduction, Report Prepared As Part Of TCRP Project J-11/Tasks Transit Cooperative Research Program, Transportation Research Board Submitted To American Public Transportation Association in http://www.apta.com/research/into/online/land_use.cfmi, accessed 17 April 2008.

The UK Standing Advisory Committee On Trunk Road Assessment (SACTRA) (1999). Transport And The Economy (Report To UK DETR). Retrieved From: http://webarchive.nationalarchives.gov.uk/20050301192906 ; http://dft.gov.uk/stellent/groups/dft-econappr/documents/pdf/dft_econappr_pdf_022512.pdf

Wikipedia Contributors (2008). Arterial Roads In Wikipedia, The Free Encyclopeda, http://en.wikipedia.org/w/index.php?title=Arterial_road&oldid=212832640(accessed May30,2008).

THREE

Future Developed Countries Need What Living Change

Reducing global environmental pollution advantages

What are the advantages to reduce global environmental pollution to our future societies? If we do not continue to avoid to cause air and water pollution from manufacture or driving car etc. business or enjoyment activities, what negative influences what are caused to our future societies? I shall attempt to explain as below:

Firstly , I shall discuss whether reducing greenhouse gases benefits air quality how and why it can save human future lives. Air quality "co-benefits" result mainly from reductions in air pollutant emissions from the same sources that emit greenhouse gases. For example, replacing a coal-fired power plant with a renewable electricity source, such as wind power, reduces both air pollutant and greenhouse gas emissions. Nowadays, our world has been slow to adopt significant actions to address climate change, as it is a long-term and global problem. The benefits of reducing carbon dioxide today are felt in the future, and since they occur globally, countries may take little action and rely on others to lead. On the other hand, better air quality and improved health are realized rapidly and locally, providing government leaders with tangible benefits from their actions to reduce carbon dioxide. For example, reducing greenhouse gases pollution , it can bring health benefits of Air Pollution Reduction to influence global has more fresh air to let we can breathe, then we can avoid air pollution breath to cause our lung hurt, even death easily. Air pollution is a grave risk to human health that affects nearly everyone in the world and nearly every organ in the body. Fortunately, it is largely a preventable risk. Reducing pollution at its source can have a rapid and substantial impact on health. Within a few weeks, respiratory and irritation symptoms, such as shortness of breath, cough, phlegm, and sore throat, disappear; school absenteeism, clinic visits, hospitalizations, premature births, cardiovascular illness and death, and all-cause mortality decrease significantly. The interventions are cost-effective. Reducing factors causing air pollution and climate change have strong cobenefits. Although regions with high air pollution have the greatest potential for health benefits, health improvements continue to be associated with pollution decreases even below international standards. The large response to and short time needed for benefits of these interventions emphasize the urgency of improving global air quality and the importance of increasing efforts to reduce pollution at local levels.

- The consequences of water and air and water and chemical pollution

Air pollution may bring these effects. Diseases such as amoebiasis, typhoid and hookworm are caused by polluted drinking water.Water polluted by chemicals such as heavy metals, lead, pesticides and hydrocarbon can cause hormonal and reproductive.A polluted beach causes rashes, hepatitis, gastroenteritis, diarrhea, encephalitis, stomach aches and vomiting. Pollution or the introduction of different forms of waste materials in our environment has negative effects to the ecosystem we rely on. How does pollution affect the ecosystem? There are many kinds of pollution, but the ones that have the most impact to us are Air and Water pollution.Pollution or the introduction of different forms of waste materials in our environment has negative effects to the ecosystem we rely on. There are many kinds of pollution, but the ones that have the most impact to us are Air and Water pollution. How does pollution affect humans? Harmful gases and particles in the air come from a range of sources, including exhaust fumes from vehicles, smoke from burning coal or gas, and tobacco smoke. There are ways to limit the effects of air pollution on health, such as avoiding areas with heavy traffic. Thus, air pollutants cause less-direct health effects when they contribute to climate change. Heat waves, extreme weather, food supply disruptions, and other effects related to increased greenhouse gases can have negative impacts on human health.

There are many kinds of pollution, but the ones that have the most impact to us are Air, Water, and chemical pollution. How does pollution affect humans? In the following paragraphs, we will enumerate the consequences of releasing pollutants in the environment. We cause most of the pollution and we will suffer the consequences if we don't stop. We are already seeing its effects in the form of global warming, contaminated seafood, increased cases of lung diseases and more.

We release a variety of chemicals into the atmosphere when we burn the fossil fuels we use every day. We breathe air to live and what we breathe has a direct impact on our health. Over 100 million years of healthy life are lost every single year as a result of air pollution. On average, that's the same as 1 year and 8 months of healthy life lost for every single person on Earth.

Air pollution is the world's 4th most lethal killer

Air pollution is the cause of 8.9 million deaths globally every year. That means that every 4 seconds, someone somewhere on the planet dies from air pollution. The UN has called air pollution the world's worst environmental health risk. Air pollution is also the world's 4th most lethal killer (following malnutrition, unsafe sex, and the lack of safe, clean water and sanitation).

Air pollution from car exhaust affects human reproduction

If pregnant women are exposed to air pollution from car exhaust, it can alter the structure of the chromosomes in the fetus and increase the risks of cancer and various birth defects.

Air pollution and climate change closely linked

The main cause of air pollution as well as climate change (CO2-emissions) is the burning of fossil fuels (oil, coal, gas). A change to greener alternatives such as solar or wind power will therefore help both the climate and human health.

How air pollution influences human health

Breathing polluted air puts you at a higher risk for asthma and other respiratory diseases. When exposed to ground ozone for 6 to 7 hours, scientific evidence show that healthy people's lung function decreased and they suffered from respiratory inflammation.Air pollutants are mostly carcinogens and living in a polluted area can put people at risk of Cancer.

Coughing and wheezing are common symptoms observed on city folks.

Damages the immune system, endocrine and reproductive systems.

High levels of particle pollution have been associated with higher incidents of heart problems.The burning of fossil fuels and the release of carbon dioxide in the atmosphere are causing the Earth to become warmer. Read about the effects of Global Warming here.The toxic chemicals released into the air settle into plants and water sources. Animals eat the contaminated plants and drink the water. The poison then travels up the food chain – to us.

Water Pollution Effects

Just like the air we breathe, water is vital to our survival. We need clean water to drink, to irrigate our crops and the fish we eat live in the waters. We play in rivers, lakes and streams – we live near bodies of water. It's a precious resource that can easily be polluted and the contamination can be transferred to us and affect our health.

The consumer society is powered by water

Everything we buy, use, eat takes water to produce. Our total use of water through the stuff we buy is represented by "The water footprint". The global water footprint is 9 trillion tons per year or almost 300,000 tons per second.

The consumer society is getting more and more thirsty

Global demand for freshwater is projected to increase 55 % between 2000 and 2050. By 2050, it will reach a massive 5500 square kilometers or 5.5 trillion tons. The main sources for the rise in freshwater use are industry and manufacturing with an expected increase of 400 %. In addition, water demand from electricity-generation will increase 140 % and domestic use 130 %.

The pollution of groundwater resources is increasing

280 billion tons of groundwater is being polluted annually. In 2000, Earth's groundwater resources were being polluted twice as fast as in 1960. Water polluted by chemicals such as heavy metals, lead, pesticides and hydrocarbon can cause hormonal and reproductive problems, damage to the nervous system, liver and kidney damage and cancer – to name a few. Being exposed to mercury causes Parkinson's disease, Alzheimer's, heart disease and death. A polluted beach causes rashes, hepatitis, gastroenteritis, diarrhea, encephalitis, stomach aches and vomiting.Water pollution affects marine life which is one of our food sources. Remember the stories of contaminated shellfish and how those who ate them died?

Plastic pollution

Plastic wasn't invented until the late 1800s and the production of plastic didn't take off until around 1950. But then it really took off. The world has produced over 9 billion tons of plastic since around 1950. 6.3 billion tons (over two thirds!) of this plastic have ended up in the environment - including our oceans. By 2025, there will be a staggering 100 bags of plastic for each foot of coastline in the world! At this point, the ocean will contain around one ton of plastic for every three tons of fish. By 2050, there could be more plastic than fish (by weight) in the world's oceans. Just imagine. Diseases such as amoebiasis, typhoid and hookworm are caused by polluted drinking water.

We live in an ecosystem where the action of one has the potential to affect the many. This can be a good or a bad thing, depending on what the action is. Our mistakes has polluted the environment that we live in and we are waking up and owning to the fact. We are trying to reverse the damage. The good news is that every positive action counts. The small effort you make towards a greener environment can start a healing ripple effect. We may still save what is left of our natural resources and make the world a better place to live in for our future generation.

Chemical pollution

Global production of synthetic chemicals is around 250 billion tons a year. Many of these chemicals find their way into our bodies and the consequences are horrifying. In samples from human beings, a study found as many as 420 different chemicals known to or suspected of causing cancer.Another study found an average of 200 industrial chemicals present in the cord blood of newborn babies.

287 different chemicals were identified in the cord blood.

180 can cause cancer

217 are toxic to the brain and nervous system

208 can cause birth defects or abnormal development.

This is truly terrifying. Especially since the global production of synthetic chemicals is expected to increase six-fold between 2000 and 2050.

On average, we already have around 700 synthetic chemicals in our body that are not a natural part of the human body chemistry. And we know very little about how the combination of these chemicals will affect us.

- Reducing air and water and plastic and chemical pollution different policies implement will be needed to different countries in our future societies.

Over the last decades, energy and pollution control policies combined with structural changes in the economy decoupled emission trends from economic growth, increasingly also in the developing world. It is found that effective implementation of the presently decided national pollution control regulations should allow further economic growth without major deterioration of ambient air quality, but will not be enough to reduce pollution levels in many world regions. A combination of ambitious policies focusing on pollution controls, energy and climate, agricultural production systems and addressing human consumption habits could drastically improve air quality throughout the world. By 2040, mean population exposure to PM2.5 from anthropogenic sources could be reduced by about 75% relative to 2015 and brought well below the WHO guideline in large areas of the world. While the implementation of the proposed technical measures is likely to be technically feasible in the future, the transformative changes of current practices will require strong political will, supported by a full appreciation of the multiple benefits. Improved air quality would avoid a large share of the current 3–9 million cases of premature deaths annually. At the same time, the measures that deliver clean air would also significantly reduce emissions of greenhouse gases and contribute to multiple UN sustainable development goals.

Given the dynamics of these factors and their complex interplay, what could be expected for future air quality around the world, and which determinants will be dominating? To answer this question, this paper identifies key factors that contributed to historic air pollution trends in different world regions, outlines conceivable ranges of their future development and examines their interplay on global air quality in the next decades. In particular, the paper provides a fresh perspective on how ambitious policy interventions could achieve clean air worldwide.

● Future projections of air pollutant emissions

A range of studies in the scientific literature explored the implications of these findings on future emissions and air quality. For a long time, future global air pollutant trends were mainly modelled in the context of long-term greenhouse gas emission scenarios . The early global studies on air pollutant emissions, notably the scenarios developed for the 'Special Report on Emissions Scenarios' and the 'Representative Concentration Pathways' that have been prepared for the Intergovernmental Panel on Climate Change (IPCC) proposed declining trends of (energy-related) air pollutants, due to autonomous technological progress and assumed pollution control policies along the environmental Kuznets hypothesis. Later, the improved understanding of the importance of targeted air quality policy interventions motivated a more differentiated approach to projections of air pollutant emissions, resulting in a wider range of air pollutant trajectories than in previous global scenarios. At the same time, the climate community addressed the interactions between decarbonization strategies and air pollutant emissions, both with the interest to reveal health benefits from low carbon policies and to explore the combined impacts of long-lived greenhouse gases and short-lived air pollutants (e.g. SO2 and black carbon) on radiative forcing and temperature increase . In general, the literature reveals strong impacts of ambitious decarbonization strategies on energy-related air pollutants SO2, NOx and PM, due to the phase-out of fossil fuels and the containment of all flue gases connected with carbon capture and storage. However, enhanced use of biomass as a greenhouse gas policy measure may lead to higher PM emissions . Compared to the climate-focused analyses that deal mainly with energy-related emissions and the role of climate policy interventions, only a few studies addressed the longer-term prospects for air pollution from a health- and ecosystems perspective. These studies take full account of other sources that also contribute substantially to population exposure to harmful air pollution, such as agricultural activities, waste management and materials handling. Also, they developed a more holistic approach towards the understanding of future trends in nitrogen emissions and their health and environmental impacts.

- How air pollution may influence the course of pandemics

The COVID-19 pandemic is causing devastating mortality, with the highest rates of intensive care unit hospitalization and morbidity among older adults, men, and those with certain preexisting conditions, most notably cardiopulmonary diseases, obesity, and diabetes. In addition, a host of interrelated socioeconomic factors—including race, ethnicity, occupation, and poverty—increase the risks of COVID-19 infection for people of color, health care professionals, and other essential workers. These factors are, in turn, influenced by conditions of the human environment including chronic levels of air pollution, most notably fine particulate matter (PM2.5) that is a well-established risk factor for death from cardiovascular and pulmonary obstructive diseases. This raises the question of whether long-term exposure to higher levels of PM2.5 increases the severity of COVID-19 and, if so, what measures might be taken to ameliorate those risks. This is the challenge addressed by Wu et al. in a new contribution to a developing series of papers for Science Advances that is dedicated to the study of pandemics from an environmental perspective.The ideal way to address questions about how PM2.5 pollution might influence the course of the pandemic would involve the study of detailed health datasets for very large numbers of people from all walks of life and locations. In this way, the potential effects of PM2.5 pollution might be evaluated in the context of other details about each individual's life history and conditions. The amount of time required for rigorous, extensive studies, however, conflicts with the swift nature of the COVID-19 pandemic. Addressing the potential impact of air pollution on COVID-19 mortality requires a more nimble approach to environmental policy decision-making.

COVID-19–related death counts (compiled by Johns Hopkins University for more than 3000 U.S. counties) and well-established PM2.5 pollution levels for each county. The results show that higher values of exposure to PM2.5 are positively correlated with higher county-level mortality after taking into account over 20 potentially confounding factors. Most notably, they conclude that an increase of just 1 μg/m3 in the long-term average of pollution is associated with a significant 11% increase in a county's rate of mortality.There are strong policy implications for these results. COVID-19, zoonotic influenza, and other potentially severe emerging zoonotic diseases are and will remain long-term threats to our species. Rapidly emerging datasets suggest that these threats are likely to be exacerbated by air pollution, even at the levels currently attained in the United States despite conscientious efforts to improve air quality. While incomplete and not yet fully vetted by the broader scientific community, pathfinding studies such as that of Wu et al. set the stage for more traditional environmental epidemiology research.

● Benefits of Reducing and Reusing policy

Recucing and reusing policy may help our earth to avoid serious pollution influences , such as prevents pollution caused by reducing the need to harvest new raw materials, saves energy, reduces greenhouse gas emissions that contribute to global climate change, helps sustain the environment for future generations, reduces the amount of waste that will need to be recycled or sent to landfills and incinerators and allows products to be used to their fullest extent.

● Ideas on How to Reduce and Reuse to implement

Buy used. You can find everything from clothes to building materials at specialized reuse centers and consignment shops. Often, used items are less expensive and just as good as new. Look for products that use less packaging. When manufacturers make their products with less packaging, they use less raw material. This reduces waste and costs. These extra savings can be passed along to the consumer. Buying in bulk, for example, can reduce packaging and save money. Buy reusable over disposable items. Look for items that can be reused; the little things can add up. For example, you can bring your own silverware and cup to work, rather than using disposable items.

Maintain and repair products, like clothing, tires and appliances, so that they won't have to be thrown out and replaced as frequently. Borrow, rent or share items that are used infrequently, like party decorations, tools or furniture.

Thus, we are living in our earth. We are everyone has responsibilities to do environmental protection activities in every day, such as reduce and reuse activity will be our right environmental protection daily behavior, walking replaces to reducing to driving when we need short time to arrive the destination in any time, manufacturers need to buy air and water clean machines to avoid serious air and water pollution in their factory manufacturing processes, we need to reduce the frequeny to travel, e.g. one to two times travelling by air planes every year, then sky will have much fresh air in our earth, also airlines need to shorten flying time , e.g. New Zealand airlines only fly to Australia near distance country , it can not fly to US, or UK far away distance countries, China airlines only fly to Singapore, Japan etc. near distance Asia countries, they do not fly to US, UK far away disrance countries. Then, our future environment pollution will be reduced as well as we can have much fresh air to breathe and drive clean water to proplong our lives when we have health.

Improving internet technology development

Why do we improve to improve internet technology? What long term social benefits will benefits if scientists can improve internet speed and reseach any information function ? I shall research these questions to give suggestion as below:

Why does internet improvement make life better? Internet of Things Benefits In short, the scale of change that IoT technology offers can be scary. At the same time, the benefits of a well-executed IoT strategy can be more need for an organization: Safety, Comfort, Efficiency. Also, the Internet offers teens the ability to make friends with peers with whom they would not otherwise connect. With pop culture deteriorating into many distinct subcultures, teens' interests are more variable than they have ever been.With internet communication, employees can effortlessly communicate with one another at anytime from anywhere in the world. This allows employees situated in different parts of the world to give their opinion and voice their concerns. Through internet access, individuals in developing countries are able to gain access to more of the modern economy. With internet connectivity, those living in remote areas can now easily take out microloans, participate in e-banking and more. A large share of respondents predict enormous potential for improved quality of life over the next 50 years for most individuals thanks to internet connectivity, although many said the benefits of a wired world are not likely to be evenly distributed.

- How internet can excite young to learn?

Internet can learn youngs to learn much different new knowlege when they research any questions and find answers from internet channel.

As one major aspect of teen life is social environment, changes in how teens connect impact the ways in which teens develop social skills. ** Luckily, the Internet offers many social-skill enhancement opportunities for teens of all different personalities . One advantage the Internet brings that the standard school environment cannot is the ability for teens to adjust their amount of social interaction. Teens who are extremely outgoing can spend their free time in social environments both offline and online, making new connections and catching up with friends.For example, a teen who finds large amounts of face-to-face interaction to be intimidating can use the Internet to engage in conversations while reducing the potential for social anxiety. In a way, this trains less social teens to be more social . In the past, these types of teens did not have the advantage of this social training provided by the Internet.

● Internet can encourage Social Network Growth

The Internet offers teens the ability to make friends with peers with whom they would not otherwise connect. With pop culture deteriorating into many distinct subcultures, teens' interests are more variable than they have ever been. Whereas in the past, children at school might have discussed the current top 40 when discussing music, today's kids define their musical tastes as specific genres, such as post-industrial, dubstep or jpop. Today, it's harder for teens to find peers who share the same interests in their schools. But online, not so. The Internet's social networks help teens find communities of peers who share similar interests, allowing a teen to grow his social network in a way that is specific to him 2. Today's teens are increasingly willing to make friends with different groups of people due to the ability to actually meet them, and this can be useful when they reach adulthood, a time in which accepting people of different backgrounds and demographics is crucial to career and academic growth. The Internet offers teens the ability to make friends with peers with whom they would not otherwise connect.

Today's teens are increasingly willing to make friends with different groups of people due to the ability to actually meet them, and this can be useful when they reach adulthood, a time in which accepting people of different backgrounds and demographics is crucial to career and academic growth.But the Internet can help teens foster self identity through exposure to new people, communities, hobbies and concepts. As teens go through more experiences, they learn more about themselves. And as the Internet can offer teens a wealth of experience, it can play the role of hastening the development of self identity.For many teens, the hardest part of life is figuring out identity.But the Internet can help teens foster self identity through exposure to new people, communities, hobbies and concepts.

● What Are Main Benefits of Internet Communication speed improvement ?

It may include as below:

1 Makes communication easier

Doing business through phone or mail doesn't work well ? Before the internet came into existence, the only way to communicate was through a phone. Or if you needed to send a note you had to send letters via mail. With the arrival of the Internet, staff and team managers can connect instantaneously without leaving their work place. ezTalks Meetings, a one-stop internet communication provider, is a perfect example. With this platform, participants can communicate as if they were right next to one another thanks to its quality video and audio. The tool comes with a rich set of features like screen sharing, cross platform chat, innovative whiteboard, and more.

2 Enhances collaboration

Internet communication brings teams together across the globe. Staff can collaborate easily without limitations and make more informed decisions instantaneously. This leads to reduced project timelines, cutting back on the time required to launch a new product/service. This piece of technology is also useful in education. Not only can students collaborate with foreign students, they can share ideas and learn about the diverse cultures out there. Parents can also become actively involved in their kids education by linking their children school with libraries, homes, and more. Millions of schools around the world are already using this technology to enhance learning.

3 It is cost effective

The cost of internet communication is significantly low when compared with other means of communication like face to face meetings and mail delivery. The technology connects you to your partners, colleagues, clients and suppliers from just about any location for a fraction of the cost required to host a one-on-one meeting. And as technology continues to become more efficient, the cost of online communication continues to drop significantly. With the traditional face to face meeting, you need to spare time, cash to travel and so on. Internet communication allows you and your team to connect without having to leave your offices.

4 Improves work relationships

Building a good relationship between workers spread around the globe is not easy. Business trips can negatively affect life– work balance. Team members can burn out fast if they have to make business travels that deny them the chance to participate in crucial events with friends and family. With internet communication, employees can effortlessly communicate with one another at anytime from anywhere in the world. This allows employees situated in different parts of the world to give their opinion and voice their concerns. Therefore, internet communication is an important business asset, particularly for companies that have tapped into global markets.

5 Increases productivity

While the companies of yesteryear might not have treasured effective communication, modern workplace requires both the management and the staff have the tools to effectively communicate internally and externally. This is because effective communication is important in increasing productivity as it directly impacts the behavior of the employees and how they perform. Internet communication plays an integral role in getting stuff done fast and efficiently which ultimately improves productivity. Poor communication can have a negative effect on productivity as the staff may not get the adequate info to accomplish a job they have been assigned.

6 Increases accountability

Errors slow down productivity and so it is tempting to punish or fire employees who repeatedly make errors. One major advantage of internet communication is that it helps to decrease these errors. This piece of technology pinpoints errors and how staff can avoid them. In workplaces that don't make use of various forms of internet communication, those mistakes go unnoticed. With internet communication, there is no room for mistakes as employees feel liable for their actions and safe to point out mistakes. They also feel secure expressing their ideas and suggestions in a group setting.

● Why does internet improvement can help any industries services or efficiencies improvment?

Internet improvement will revolutionize the world and lead to groundbreaking changes in transportation, industry, communication, education, energy, health care, communication, entertainment, government, warfare and even basic research. For example, self-driving cars, trains, semi-trucks, ships and airplanes will mean that goods and people can be transported farther, faster and with less energy and with massively fewer vehicles. Automated mining and manufacturing will further reduce the need for human workers to engage in rote work. Machine language translation will finally close the language barrier, while digital tutors, teachers and personal assistants with human qualities will make everything from learning new subjects to booking salon appointments faster and easier. For businesses, automated secretaries, salespeople, waiters, waitress, baristas and customer support personnel will lead to cost savings, efficiency gains and improved customer experiences. Socially, individuals will be able to find AI pets, friends and even therapists who can provide the love and emotional support that many people so desperately want. Entertainment will become far more interactive, as immersive AI experiences come to supplement traditional passive forms of media. Energy generation and health care will vastly improve with the addition of powerful AI tools that can take a systems-level view of operations and locate opportunities to gain efficiencies in design and operation. AI-driven robotics (e.g., drones) will revolutionize warfare. Finally, intelligent AI will contribute immensely to basic research and likely begin to create scientific discoveries of its own. So, it implies that internet improvement ought assist any kinds of industy service or efficiency improvement.

- Internet may become any organizational digital assets

On an individual basis, we will think about our digital assets as much as our physical ones. Ideally, we will have more transparent control over our data, and the ability to understand where it resides and exchange it for value – negotiating with the platform companies that are now in a winner-take-all position. Some children born today are named with search engine-optimization in mind; we'll be thinking more comprehensively about a set of rights and responsibilities of personal data that children are born with. Governments will have a higher level of regulation and protection of individual data. On an individual level, there will be greater integration of technology with our physical selves. For example, I can see devices that augment hearing and vision, and that enable greater access to data through our physical selves. Hard for me to picture what that looks like, but 50 years is a lot of time to figure it out. On a societal level, AI will have affected many jobs. Not only the truck drivers and the factory workers, but professions that have been largely unassailable – law, medicine – will have gone through a painful transformation. It seems entirely reasonable that a great deal of our digital lives will be focused on habitable environments: identifying them, improving them, expanding them.

Significant, often highly communication and computation technologically driven, advances in day-to-day areas like health care, safety and human services, will continue to have a significant measurable improvement in many lives, often 'invisible' as an unnoticed reduction in bad outcomes, will continue to reduce the incidence of human-scale disasters. Advances in opportunities for self-actualisation through education, community and creative work will continue. So, I believe that future many organizations may apply internet communication tool for their digital assets.

- Internet improvement may assist robotic development

Most of the focus on technology and particularly AI and machine learning developments these days is limited to virtual systems (e.g., apps for travel booking, social networks, search engines, games). I expect this to move, in the next 50 years, into networking people with machines, remotely operating in a myriad of environments, such as homes, hospitals, factories, sport arenas and so on. This will change work as we know it today, as it will change medicine (increasing remote surgery), travel (autonomous and remotely-guided cars, trains, planes), entertainment (games where real robots, instead of virtual agents, evolve in real scenarios). These are just a few ideas/scenarios. Many more, difficult to anticipate today, will appear. They will bring further challenges on privacy, security and safety, which everyone should be closely watching and monitoring. Beyond current discussions on privacy problems concerning 'virtual world' apps, we need to consider that 'real world' apps may enhance many of those problems, as they interact physically and/or in proximity with humans. So, future historians will observe that, in many ways, the rise of the internet over the next few decades will have improved the world, but it hasn't been without its costs that were sometimes severe and disruptive to entire industries and nations as well as improve robotic development.

This is similarly valid for AI.Living longer and better lives is the shining promise of the digital age. Many respondents to this canvassing agreed that internet advancement is likely to lead to better human-health outcomes, although perhaps not for everyone. As the following comments show, experts foresee new cures for chronic illnesses, rapid advancement in biotechnology and expanded access to care thanks to the development of better telehealth systems. Life will improve in multiple ways. One in particular I think worth mentioning will be improvements in health care in three distinct ways. One is significantly better medical technology related to cancer and other major diseases. The second is significantly reduced cost of health care. The third is much higher and broader availability of high-quality health care, thereby reducing the differences in outcomes between wealthy and poor citizens. So, when hospitals can improve internet communication , if the hospital can apply robots to assist doctors and nurses to serve patients. Then, internet communication can help them to cooperate more efficient.

- Internet improvement to assist 5G laptop development

Many of the technologies we see commercialized today began in government and university research labs. Fifty years ago, computers were the size of walk-in closets, and the notion of personal computers was laughable to most people. Today we're facing another shift, from personal and mobile to ambient computing. We're also seeing a huge amount of research in the areas of prosthetics, neuroscience and other technologies intended to translate brain activity into physical form. All discussion of transhumanism aside, there are very real current and future applications for technology 'implants' and prosthetics that will be able to aid mobility, memory, even intelligence, and other physical and neurological functions.

And, as nearly always happens, the technology is far ahead of our understanding of the human implications. Will these technologies be available to all, or just to a privileged class? What happens to the data? Will it be 'willed' as a digital legacy to future generations? What are the ethical (and for some, religious and spiritual) implications of changing the human body with technology? In many ways, these are not new questions. We've used technology to augment the physical form since the first caveman picked up a walking stick. But the key here will be to focus as much (or more) on the way we use these technologies as we do on inventing them. All of above factors will be influenced to future 5G mobile phone by internet improvement?

Our homes, transportation, appliances, communication devices and even our clothes will be constantly communicating as part of a digital network. We have enough pieces of this today that we can somewhat imagine what it will be like. Through our clothes, doctors can monitor in real time our vital signs, metabolic condition and markers relevant to specific diseases. Parents will have real-time information about young children. The difference in the future will be the constant sharing of information, data updates and responses of all these interconnected devices. The things we create will interact with us to protect us. Our notions of privacy and even liability will be redefined. Lowering the cost and increasing the effectiveness of health care will require sharing information about how our bodies are functioning. Those who opt out may have to accept palliative hospice care over active treatment. Not keeping track of children real-time may be considered a form of child neglect. Digital will do more than connect our things to each other – it will invade our bodies. Advances in prosthetics, replacement organs and implants will turn our bodies into digital devices. This will create a host of new issues, including defining 'human' and where the line exists between that human and the digital universe – if people are always connected, always on are humans now part of the internet?

● How internet improvement influences AI provides medical service to hospitals?

Similarly, AI embedded in devices or wearables can be applied to predict and ameliorate many mental health illnesses. However, there is potential for there to be huge inequalities in our societies in the ability of individuals to access such technologies, causing both social disruption and new causes for mental health diseases, such as depression and anxiety. On balance, I am an optimist about the ability of human beings to adjust and develop new ethical norms for dealing with such issues.Surveillance technology, especially that powered by AI algorithms, is becoming more powerful and all-present than ever before. But to look at that and say that technology won't help people is absurd. Medical technology, technology to help people with disabilities, technology that will increase our comfort and abilities as humans will continue to appear and develop.The digital revolution will bring benefits in particular for health, providing personalized monitoring through Internet of Things and wearable devices. The AI will analyze those data in order to provide personalized medicine solutions.The most noticeable change for better in the next 50 years will be in health and average life expectancy. At this pace, and, taking into account the developments in digital technologies, I hope that several discoveries will reduce the risk of death, such as cancer or even death by road accident. New drugs could be developed, increasing the active work age and possibility maintaining the sustainability of countries' social health care and retirement funds. Another area AI can have impact is in creating the framework within genomics, epigenomics and metabolomics can be used to keep people healthy and to intervene when we start to deviate from health. Indeed, with AI we may be able to hack the brain and other secreting cells so that we can auto-generate lifesaving medicines, block unwanted biological processes (e.g., cancer), and coupled to understanding the brain, be able to hack at neurological disorders."

Thus, I believe that future hospitals were able to utilize internet technology to solve human health problems to make citizens' lives better and improve their access to care and services to improve their health outcomes. The benefits of the internet in the health care industry have continued to improve access to care and services, particularly for elderly, disabled or rural citizens. Digital tools will continue to be integrated into daily life to help the most vulnerable and isolated who need services, care and support. With laws supporting these groups, benefits in these areas will continue and expand to include behavioral health and resources for this group and for others. In the area of behavioral health in particular, digital tools will provide far-reaching benefits to citizens who need services but do not access them directly in person. Access to behavioral health will increase significantly in the next 50 years as a result of more enhanced and widely available digital tools made available to practitioners for delivering care to vulnerable populations, and by minimizing the stigma of accessing this type of care in person. It is a more affordable, personalized and continuous way of providing this type of care that is also more likely to attain adherence.

● The cyborg generation: Humans will partner more directly with technology when internet is popular to be used in any where

The inevitable 'Singularity' will result in changes to humans and will increase the rate of our evolution toward hybrid 'machines.' I also believe that new and modified materials will become 'smart.' For instance, new materials will be 'self-aware' and will be able to communicate problems in order to avoid failure. Ultimately, these materials will become 'self-healing' and will be able to harness raw materials to manufacture replacement parts in situ. All these materials, and the things built with them will participate in the connected world. We will see continued blurring of the line between 'real' and 'virtual' life." For exaple, artificial general intelligence and quantum computing available in a future version of the cloud connected to individual brain augmentation could make us augmented geniuses, inventing our daily lives in a self-actualization economy as the conscious-technology civilization evolves. Implants in humans that continuously connect them to the web will lead to a loss of privacy and the potential for thought control, decline in autonomy.

● Everyone agrees that the world will be putting AI to work, when internet is improvement to raise robotic efficiency and performance improvement

The technology visionaries surveyed described a much different work environment from the current one. They say remote work arrangements are likely to be the rule, rather than the exception, and virtual assistants will handle many of the mundane and unpleasant tasks currently performed by humans. The shooting is done by a drone guided by a smart guy/gal working a 9-to-5 job in an air-conditioned office in a nice town. Garbage could be picked up, sorted, recycled, all by robots with AI. Tedious surgery completed by robots and teaching via YouTube would leave the humans to the interesting and exciting cases, not the redoing of same lessons to yet more patients/students. Humans could live well on a 20-hour work week with many weeks of paid vacation. Having a job/career could become a positive, not just a necessity. With 24/7 learning and just-in-time capacity, people could change areas or careers many times with ease whenever they become bored. This positive outcome is possible if we collectively manage the creation and distribution of the tools and access to the use of new emerging tools. Thus, future everyone will have hundreds of digital workers working for them. Our cognitive mediators will know us in some ways better than we know ourselves. Better episodic memories and large numbers of digital workers will allow expanded entrepreneurship, lifelong learning and focus on transformation.

Thus, our future social development already small world will shrink further as remote collaboration becomes the norm, resulting in major social changes, among them allowing the recent concentration of expertise in major cities to relax and reducing the relevance of national borders. Furthermore, deep learning and AI-assisted technologies for software development and verification, combined with more abstract primitives for executing software in the cloud, will enable even those not trained as software engineers to precisely describe and solve complex problems. I believe the question we're facing is not 'When will machines surpass human intelligence?' but instead 'How can humans work together with machines in new ways?' Rather than worrying about an impending Singularity, I propose the concept of Multiplicity: where diverse combinations of people and machines work together to solve problems and innovate. In analogy with the 1910 High School Movement that was spurred by advances in farm automation, I propose a 'Multiplicity Movement' to evolve the way we learn to emphasize the uniquely human skills that AI and robots cannot replicate: creativity, curiosity, imagination, empathy, human communication, diversity and innovation. AI systems can provide universal access to sophisticated adaptive testing and exercises to discover the unique strengths of each student and to help each student amplify his or her strengths. AI systems could support continuous learning for students of all ages and abilities. Rather than discouraging the human workers of the world with threats of an impending Singularity, let's focus on Multiplicity where advances in AI and robots can inspire us to think deeply about the kind of work we really want to do, how we can change the way we learn and how we might embrace diversity to create myriad new partnerships. So, future AI and internet technoloy will become new partners to assist any business development, even any organizations and social development. Hence, internet improvement must be needed in order to let any businesses can apply robots to raise efficiencies and improve performance more effectively. For example, free internet-connected devices will be available to the poor in exchange for carrying around a sensor that records traffic speed, environmental quality, detailed usage logs, and video and audio recordings (depending on state law). There will be secure vote-by-internet capabilities, through credit card or passport verification, with other secure kiosks available at public facilities (police stations, libraries, fire stations and post offices, should those continue to exist in their current form). Internet and 24/7 real-time connectivity will no longer be viewed as a 'thing' independent from daily life, but integral, like electricity. This has profound psychological implications about what people assume as normal and establishes baseline expectations for access, response times and personalization of functions and information. Contrary to many concerns, as technology becomes more sophisticated, it will ultimately support the primary human drives of social connectedness and agency. As we have seen with social media, first adoption is noncritical – it is a shiny penny for exploration. Then people start making judgments about the value-add based on their own goals and technology companies adapt by designing for more value to the user . Technology is going to change whether we like it or not – expecting it to be worse for individuals means that we look for what's wrong. Expecting it to be better means we look for the strengths and what works and work toward that goal. Technology gives individuals more control – a fundamental human need and a prerequisite to participatory citizenship and collective agency. The danger is that we are so distracted by technology that we forget that digital life is an extension of the offline world and demands the same critical, moral and ethical thinking.

In future 50 years every aspect of our life will be connected, organized and hence, partly controlled, as technology platform and applications businesses will take this opportunity. A few global players will dominate the business; smaller companies (startups) will mostly have a chance in the development sector. Many institutions, such as libraries, will disappear – there might be one or two libraries that function as museums to show how it used to be. People who experienced today's world will definitely value the benefits and amenities they have through technology (human-machine/AI collaboration). If technology becomes part of every aspect of our lives we will have to give up some power and control. People thinking in today's terms will lose a certain amount of freedom, independency and control over their lives. People born after 2030 will probably just think these technologies produced changes that are mostly for the better. It has always been like this – people have always thought/said 'in the old days everything was better. The free, open internet that represented a set of decentralized connections between idiosyncratic actors will be recognized as an aberration in the history of the internet. Today's internet giants will probably be the internet giants of 50 years from now. In recent years, they've made substantial progress in curtailing innovation through acquisitions and copying. As the industry matures, they will add regulatory capture to their skill sets. For many people around the world, the internet will be a set of narrow portals where they exchange their data for a curtailed set of communication, information and consumer services. Thus, digital tools will be part of our body inside and remotely, and will assist us in decision- making constantly, so it will become second nature. Nonetheless, physical feelings will still be exclusively 'physical,' i.e., there will be a significant difference between the 'sensor-based feelings' and real body feelings, so human beings will still have some advantages over technology. This, I believe, will last forever.

Discovery new health medicine drugs

Why do we need to concern new health medicine drugs discovery? I believe that human will face any new kinds of diseases that we had not encountered or contacts in my past. If we lack any new kinds of health medicine drugs discovery to fight any kinds of new diseases in my future. Then, we must face death very easily, such as COVID 19 is one kind of new disease, the another person or other persons can be contacted to cause this kind of COVID 19 disease by the patient's cloths, shoes, hands, even air, mouth of hs body and things. Thus, it had caused many people die in global nowadays. So, medicine or drug or bio-scientists need to spend much time to do any experiment to attempt to discover any new kinds of medicines or drugs to fight any future new kinds of diseases. Otherwise, human will die very easily in soon.

● Why do we need drug discovery?

In the fields of medicine, biotechnology and pharmacology, drug discovery is the process by which new candidate medications are discovered. Historically, drugs were discovered by identifying the active ingredient from traditional remedies or by serendipitous discovery, as with penicillin. More recently, chemical libraries of synthetic small molecules, natural products or extracts were screened in intact cells or whole organisms to identify substances that had a desirable therapeutic effect in a process known as classical pharmacology. After sequencing of the human genome allowed rapid cloning and synthesis of large quantities of purified proteins, it has become common practice to use high throughput screening of large compounds libraries against isolated biological targets which are hypothesized to be disease-modifying in a process known as reverse pharmacology. Hits from these screens are then tested in cells and then in animals for efficacy.

However, modern drug discovery involves the identification of screening hits, medicinal chemistry and optimization of those hits to increase the affinity, selectivity (to reduce the potential of side effects), efficacy/potency, metabolic stability (to increase the half-life), and oral bioavailability. Once a compound that fulfills all of these requirements has been identified, the process of drug development can continue. If successful, clinical trials are developed. Modern drug discovery is thus usually a capital-intensive process that involves large investments by pharmaceutical industry corporations as well as national governments (who provide grants and loan guarantees). Despite advances in technology and understanding of biological systems, drug discovery is still a lengthy, "expensive, difficult, and inefficient process" with low rate of new therapeutic discovery. For example, in 2010, the research and development cost of each new molecular entity was about US$1.8 billion In the 21st century, basic discovery research is funded primarily by governments and by philanthropic organizations, while late-stage development is funded primarily by pharmaceutical companies or venture capitalists. However, discovering drugs that may be a commercial success, or a public health success, involves a complex interaction between investors, industry, academia, patent laws, regulatory exclusivity, marketing and the need to balance secrecy with communication. Meanwhile, for disorders whose rarity means that no large commercial success or public health effect can be expected, the orphan drug funding process ensures that people who experience those disorders can have some hope of pharmacotherapeutic advances.

● Where do new drugs come from? Why does it take so long to get a new drug approved? Why are drugs so expensive?

The medicines we ingest, inject, and inhale are often complex therapeutic compounds. The drugs are usually mixtures of chemicals made from starting materials or drug sources. Depending on the sources from which the drugs were created, the drugs can be categorized as natural, synthetic, or semi-synthetic. Natural drugs are made from compounds found in nature. The most prevalent natural drug sources are plants. The field of science that studies the relationship between people and medicinal plants is known as medicinal ethnobotany. Some examples of medicine that come from plants are morphine (from opium), digoxin (from flower, Digitalis lanata), and aspirin (from willow tree bark). Less prevalent natural drug sources include animals, microbes, and minerals. The first kind drug source is for example, synthetic drugs come from starting materials that are not found in nature. Instead, they are produced by man from smaller chemical building blocks. An example of synthetic medicine is the experimental anti-malaria drug, arterolane. Another kind drug source is semi-synthetic drugs are neither completely natural nor completely synthetic. They are a hybrid. Semi-synthetic drugs are generally made by converting starting materials from natural sources into final products via chemical reactions. Examples of semi-synthetic medicine include the antibiotic, penicillin, and the chemotherapy drug, paclitaxel. To make the chemotherapy drug, paclitaxel, 10-deacetylbaccatin is extracted from yew needles and undergoes a 4-stage synthesis process. They both are the main kinds of drugs manufacturing sources.

● Why does human need new drugs discovery ?

The reason of global health needs demand new approach to drug discovery, the pharmaceutical industry has made enormous strides in the production of potential therapies and medicines. But even today, close to 90% of candidate drugs that enter Phase 1 trials fail to make it to the market place. This is a system beset by duplication of effort and hence wastage of resources. No one lab or institution can do this on its own. We must urgently pool resources and expertise, minimise duplication, explore new drug targets, biomarkers, and technologies in order to generate new, effective, and more affordable drugs for patients more quickly.

Discovey of any one kind of new drug, it needs long time to experiment. It must come up with new ways to accelerate our drug discovery process. Alternatively, we must entirely rethink how we treat illness. This is not just limited to bacterial infections. We need to invent better ways to combat all forms of disease. The process of discovering, testing, and approving a drug for commercial use can take 20 years and over of 1 billion dollars. Obviously, decreasing both the time and the cost of developing these drugs can save many lives. There are some new technologies which are already helping to ramp up this process. For example, computational modeling of drugs has massively sped up the screening process for drugs. We can now take thousands of potential drug candidates and narrow them down to a couple viable options. But there are more ways we can expedite this process.

A recent estimate states that we now know the molecular cause of over 4,000 diseases — but we only have drugs for about 250. How can we do better? The FDA approval process is long and arduous. Even for compounds that have been approved in other countries, FDA trials can be drawn out for years. The FDA approval process can be responsible for about 25% of the cost of a drug and can delay the arrival of a drug over 10 years. There is even data that suggests that the FDA kills many more by not approving drugs than it ever saves by approving drugs (for more on the harmful effects of the FDA, see Cato, Forbes, The Independent Institute, and LifeExtension). By delaying good drugs that can save lives, and by doing little to stop bad drugs, the FDA is often an inhibitor to the medical process. We need to rethink the FDA if we want to streamline the drug discovery process. If we can change many FDA policies, we will see more drugs created for those 4,000 known targets.

● The process of new drug experiment success time evaluation

Any new kind of drugs experiment success, they must experience these processes. They may include:

1 Drug testing and licensing

All new drugs and treatments have to be thoroughly tested before they are licensed and available for patients. A new drug is first studied in the laboratory. If it looks promising, it is carefully studied in people. If trials show that it works well and doesn't cause too many side effects, it may be licensed. You may hear this process called 'from bench to bedside. There is no typical length of time it takes for a drug to be tested and approved. It might take 10 to 15 years or more to complete all 3 phases of clinical trials before the licensing stage. But this time span varies a lot. There are many factors that affect how long it takes for a drug to be licensed.

2 Factors that affect how long trials take

The type of cancer drug success experiement needs time

Clinical trials for rarer cancers often take longer because there are fewer patients available to take part. Research teams from several different countries may need to collaborate so there are enough patients. This can mean the trial takes longer to organise and set up. But international trials can often recruit people more quickly and so are likely be quicker in the long run.

Researchers running clinical trials for more common cancers are generally able to find enough people to take part more easily.

3 The type of treatment

Trials that use new methods of giving treatment, such as a new way to give radiotherapy for example, may take longer to set up and run. This is because the research teams need specialist equipment and extra training. These trials may only be able to run in a small number of hospitals compared to trials using standard ways of giving treatment. How long treatment takes can also affect the results. It is likely to be quicker to get results for a trial looking at a single dose or short course of treatment, compared to a treatment that lasts for months or even years.

4 The type of trial

Some trials look at treatments to prevent cancer or ways of screening for cancer. Screening means testing for cancer in people who don't have any signs or symptoms. People who join these trials haven't been diagnosed with cancer. The research team will often want to follow them for many years to see who develops cancer and who doesn't. They will then compare the different trial groups to see if a particular treatment can help prevent cancer or whether a test can help to diagnose it early.These trials often take a long time to get results compared to treatment trials. It can take years to see a clear difference in the number of people in the different groups who go on to develop cancer. So, any new kinds of drug research experiements, they depend on the number of patients needed in order to decide whether how drug quality level, how many drugs manufacturing supply number, drug price in global market.

Statistics experts look at what the research team want to find out and the design of the trial, and then work out how many patients are needed. If there aren't enough patients taking part, the results may not be reliable. The number of people they need to get reliable results will depend on how many treatment groups there are and exactly what the research team want to find out.

5 The follow up period

Research teams look at how well people are doing for some time after they have treatment as part of a trial. This is to see how well the treatment works over a longer period of time, and to find out more about long term side effects. Follow up periods can range from a few months to more than 10 years, depending on the type of treatment and the group of patients. Or maybe longer for a trial looking at screening or prevention.

6 Any problems with the new treatment

There may be problems with new drugs or treatments that the researchers don't know about until they run the trials. There could be unexpected side effects or reactions to treatment. Or there may be difficulties in giving the treatment to patients. Problems with the new treatment may mean the trial takes longer to complete.

Thus, any kinds of new drug experiement need long time to be attempted to carry on, every new kind of drug experiment is evaluated about 10 to 20 , even more time. So, future drug scientists have responsibilities to evaluate whether which kinds of diseases will cause in order to concentrate on spending time to carry on researching the kind of new drug experiment. It aims to use limited resource and time to let patients to get health.

Improving living environment

What are the disadvantages if we do not concern how to improve our global living environment? I shall explain as below:

- reasons to improve living environment

Nowadays, as population on the earth keeps expanding, human needs increase endlessly causing more global environmental problems to proliferate globally. Global environmental crisis has become an unequivocal fact that can affect our livelihood and it is capable of changing the current landscape drastically. Hence, people hold the responsibility to tackle current global environmental issues to make this world a better place. With destructive natural disasters like flash floods or snowstorm as well as the changing of weather patterns, the earth is poised at the precarious verge of severe environmental crisis. Human intervention has caused many dysfunctions to the environment, some of which have left damages on the ecosystem that eliminates other sources of necessity to other living things. Ever since humans start to harvest the Earth 's resources, many landscapes have been altered to fit the lifestyles of countless inhabitants. So people ought to be aware of other types of environmental challenges that the planet is facing. Some of the challenges that the planet is facing include overpopulation of human beings that leads to natural resources depletion, deforestation and loss of biodiversity, acid rain and ocean acidification, pollution and waste disposal. Thus, it seems that global living environment and pollution have close relationship. I mean that air and water and paste and chemical pollution will reduce if we can keep our global living environment more clean, safe and without more rubblishs are allowed to keep in our living places, even gardens, public places anywhere.

One of the key ethical questions is whether a life-extension pill would extend our healthy years or simply prolong frailty towards the end of life. Better health and longer life would certainly be an attractive prospect for many people. If we were healthier for longer then perhaps we could achieve more of our ambitions and engage in the things we enjoy for longer. But some people worry that our lives may be extended in a state of low quality of life rather than health. Although this is not the goal, critics worry that it might be an unintended consequence of intervention in ageing and longevity. As with all pharmaceuticals, both health benefits and risks need to be considered. If life span could be extended a great deal – perhaps to more than 100 years or even longer – then some other interesting issues might arise. For instance, would we simply run out of things to do and become bored? Even things that we enjoy may become stale after several centuries. How long would we have to work for? If our lives were 200 years long then it is unlikely that many people could afford to retire at 65. However, this may also present new opportunities such as having several different careers within a lifetime. If our future earth can not provide a health and clean living environment to let human to live, then our quality of living must be worse to compare nowadays, it will cause our next generation can not be health to live ot they will have many different kinds of disease, such as COV19 disease , or future there are many kinds of serious disease to compare COV19 disease , they will bring threats to influence our next generation to live in anywhere health places in our earth. It is very disappointment to us, such as our next generation's parents, we have not feel responsibilities to keep our living environment to be improved to let our next generation to live in global anywhere clean and health living environment. So, we need to concern how to improve our living environment nowadays.

However, I shall suggest these methods how to improve our living environment to be better. If we can be habit to do environment protection behaviors every day, then our living environment must be influenced to improve more easily and rapidly, in society, individual sand businessmen and our governments have resposibilities, they may include as below:

● Individual and businessmen and governments how to improve living environment

Individual responsibilities to improving living environment

1. Use Reusable Bags

Plastic grocery-type bags that get thrown out end up in landfills or in other parts of the environment. These can suffocate animals who get stuck in them or may mistake them for food. Also, it takes a while for the bags to decompose. Whether you are shopping for food, clothes or books, use a reusable bag. This cuts down on litter and prevents animals from getting a hold of them. There are even some stores (such as Target) that offer discounts for using reusable bags! These bags are useful for things other than shopping as well. I have heard of people using reusable bags when they move! If you forget your bags at home, buy a new one. Better yet, keep a couple bags in your car so you never leave home without them (just make sure you remember you put them there)! If you are in a position where you need to use the plastic bags, reuse them the next time you go shopping, or use them for something else. Just do not be so quick to throw them out!

There are some states that are outlawing or charging extra for using plastic bags. Using reusable bags helps the environment AND your budget!

2. Print as Little as Necessary

We have all had that teacher that wanted us to have a copy of every single reading when we come to class, or that professor who wanted a hard copy of the ten-page paper that is due next week. These are fine but it seems as if they do not understand that using so much paper is detrimental to the environment. What can you do? Ask your teacher if you can bring a laptop or an e-reader to class so that you can download the reading onto that and read it from there. If not, print on both sides of the page to reduce the amount of paper used. If you need to turn in a long paper, ask the professor if it is okay to print on both sides of the page and explain why you're asking. Most teachers care about the environment as well and would be willing to allow you to do so.

3. Recycle

Recycling is such a simple thing to do, but so many people don't do it. Many garbage disposal companies offer recycling services, so check with the company you use to see if they can help you get started! It is as simple as getting a bin and putting it out with your trash cans for free! Another way to recycle is to look for recycling cans near trashcans. Instead of throwing recyclables in the trash with your non-recyclables, make a point to take an extra step to locate recycling cans around your campus.

4. Use a Reusable Beverage Containers

Instead of buying individually-packaged drinks, consider buying a bulk container of the beverage you want and buying a reusable water bottle. Not only will this help the environment, but it will also help you save money since you are buying a bulk container. Many campuses offer water fountains designed for drinking as well as for refilling reusable water bottles. Make use of these fountains throughout the day when you finish off the initial beverage. Along these lines, many restaurants offer reusable containers for drinks. If you go to a certain place a lot, consider buying one of these containers to help minimize waste. A lot of coffee shops even offer a discount to customers who use a reusable container for their drinks. Starbucks, as an example, offers a small discount for customers who do this. Saving the environment and money?

5. Save Water

Water is wasted more frequently than we can see. Turn off the faucet as you are brushing your teeth. Don't turn your shower on until you're ready to get in and wash your hair. Limit your water usage as you wash dishes. Changing old habits will be good for both the environment and your wallet!

6. Avoid Taking Cars or Carpool When Possible

Cars are harmful to the environment. Taking public transportation, walking, or riding a bike to class are better options that help the environment and your budget, as well as getting some exercise in! If you do need to use your car, compare schedules and places of residency with those in your classes. You can split the cost of gas and have alternating schedules for who drives when. This is cheaper than everyone driving separately and you'll be closer with friends!

Businessmen responsibilities to improving living environment

Instead of individuals have respobsibilities to improve our living environment. Businessmen have also responsibilities to improve our living environment. I shall indicate mining businessmen example to explain how mining businesses may influence our living environment to be worse. The disadvantages of mining include harm to air pollution, water pollution, loss of usable land, destruction of animal habitat, and harm to local communities and the miners themselves. While mining produces the resources needed for fuel, electronics, and other items as well as jobs, companies often don't factor the harm mining can do into their decision making. Below factors may influence our global living environment to be worse as below:

Air Pollution

Lead, arsenic, cadmium, and other harmful substance As are often exposed by mining and picked up by the wind, causing allergies and breathing problems in local people. Mining machinery uses fossil fuels and releases large amounts of carbon dioxide and other substances that contribute to global warming.

Water Pollution

Mining can cause metal contamination and acid mine drainage that makes water unsafe for plants and animals. Sediments released by mining choke streams and erode soil. Both of these problems also cause problems for farming and the water people drink.

Loss of Usable Land

Mining, especially open pit mining, destroys land that can be used for farming, houses, and other human purposes, often permanently. Entire mountains and rivers can be destroyed. Loss of soil and deep underground excavation can also make land unstable and collapse.

Destruction of Animal Habitats

Mining also has disadvantages for plants and wildlife. It destroys homes and food sources for animals and leads to less diverse plant and animal life. Endangered species that are already sensitive to changes in their environment are especially at risk. Because mining releases toxins that linger for years later, the damage to plants and animals often isn't fully understood until after mining has ended.

Harm to Miners

Mining is dangerous for the people who do it, especially for miners who work underground. Breathing in mineral dust can cause deadly diseases like pneumoconiosis or black lung, while the machinery used often causes hearing loss. Back injuries and other physical problems are also common in miners. While big disasters often show up in the news, many of the miners who are killed or injured on the job never receive media attention. In 2010, almost 2,500 miners died from causes other than major accidents.

Consequences for Local Communities

Mining is also harmful to the communities that support mines. Mining can lead to loss of homes, land, and clean water, and it often releases chemicals into the environment that cause health problems for locals. Mines also need large amounts of water to operate, which leaves less for people to drink or farm with. It also causes less obvious problems. Because only some people in an area benefit from mining, but everyone faces at least some of the disadvantages, mining can divide communities. It can also lead to harassment or abuse from corporate or government officials who care more about the profits of mining than the people it affects. The secrecy around mining and who makes money from it often makes this disadvantage even worse.

Thus, ourselves and businessmen can not neglect our any activities can influence global living environment to be worse. We need to learn how to avoid to do any bad behaviors to influence our future global living environment to be worse, even the worst.

Governments responsibilities to improving living environment

Any country's government needs to concern social responsibility before it decides to implement any sustainable development. Because although sustainable development may bring some benefits to some countries, but it can also bring disadvantages to themselves countries. What Are Disadvantages of Sustainable Development? It may brins these disadvantages as below:

Increased Costs

Because sustainable development relies on newer technologies and materials that cost more to produce, the overall costs are often more than that of traditional construction. The higher cost of materials is passed on to developers. Developers pass it on to property owners, who pass it on to tenants. Future development will include tools that haven't even been invented yet. The trial and error of using new materials and ideas can also bring costs up for everyone.

Lower Quality of Life for Some Elements of Society

Sustainable development will shrink or do away with certain job sectors. This will lead to job loss for some workers. The fossil fuel industry could see plants close and employees lose jobs as sustainable development relies on new energy sources. The rising costs and less robust power of alternative energy can also lead to a lower quality of life for people who live in sustainably developed areas.

Resistance to New Methods

When people try to implement new ideas, there's naturally a certain amount of resistance. People in general are set in their ways and don't want to change their lives radically. As more governments and companies attempt to put sustainable development into practice, more resistance will follow.

Some of the resistance will come in the form of people who initially adopt the idea of sustainable development with enthusiasm, but their commitment shrinks as they start to put new ideas into practice. Contractors and tenants may resist a specific initiative because it forces them to change the ways they work and live.

Increased Regulation

Sustainable approaches will naturally lead to increased regulation on construction and the daily operation of businesses. A greater commitment to the environment will lead to tighter controls on how people live their lives. Stricter building codes and tougher emission standards are likely. While some people will accept a greater burden of regulation because they see the overall benefit, many people will disagree with government intruding into their lives.

Political Struggle

In addition to the public resistance, there's a political cost to committing to the environment. The deep political divides in society mean that some political powers won't want to commit to sustainable initiatives. Certain industries will try to influence politicians via lobbyists. Some politicians will be completely against sustainable development.

Is It Worth the Trouble?

People and organizations that are in favor of sustainable development believe that it's worth moving past these disadvantages to work on the environment. Advocates say that sustainable development is an investment in future generations. The biggest defenders of these initiatives are working on ways of overcoming the hurdles.

Thus, ineffective or poor sustainable development may also bring poor living environment, due to wrong sustainable development to the country. For example, if Afria government only concern how to find mining lands for sustinable development, but it neglects to keep clean and health and natural land living environment to African to continue to live. Then, it will reduce African quality of living to be worse. So, any countries governments need to keep balance to bring social benefit when they decide to do sustainable development in themselves countries.

FOUR

THE RELATIONSHIP BETWEEN SOCIAL CHANGE AND HUMAN BEHAVIOR

Human Behavioral network job brings social economic benefits

What does human network job mean ? Why may human network job be popular? Why human network job behavior may influence economy ?

Nowadays internet is popular to use. We can apply internet to find data , search any new things, even earn money. Why

does internet
may become huma network job source. For example, e-publish may be one kind of new human network job. Any authors may apply internet
channel to help them to sell electronic or paper books from e-publisher web store. They may apply facebook, you tub etc. any online
channel to promote themselves new books to let new readers to know whether when they may buy themselves favourable new topic books to read
from electronic publisher web store.

Thus, future electronic publisher industry may help any authors to build internet network platform to help them to sell and promote
ot advertise their any one new electronic or paper book topic to let global any one reader to choose to buy their any new topic books from electronic publisher web store easily and conveniently. However, it implies that electronic network platform author may be one kind of future new human network job in our societies.

How electronic network platform author job may bring economy benefit in macro economy view? A person can have few friends, contacts and still be very influential if these few
friends and contacts are themselves highly influential, e.g. one author must not need to know any one reader in global society. When they like to choose any electronic books from electronic internet network platform. They may become the author's any one topic book buyer, when they feel the author's any one topic book is fun and attract they make decision to buth the strange author whose the topic book from electronic book publisher's platform web store conventiently in short time. Although, they are strangers,

they do not know themselves , but the reader can understand what it way that made Google from writing platofrm to create new creative mind and typing network job method to replace traditional hand writing book method for global authors. It will be one kind of new human network writing job.

Hence, global any one reader can apply an innovative search engine , such as google.com to find whether whom author personal new topic books are value to read from internet.

Then, the electroniuc publisher's web store may be new book store platform sale network to help the author to sell many electronic or paper books from electronic network platform

in short time. So, internet may be future new network plaform to help global any one author to create network writing job absolutely. Furthermore, internet may be popular social media

to help any one author to build goold relationship between his/her readers. It is one kind of new network, human network job. New authors do not need to buy many paper books to prepare to put in any one book shop warehouse. Their every book can print on demand to reduce out of book stock in any one book shop. They may choose to sell either electronic books or paper books both from any one book publisher web store. So, electronic network platform may be one kind of good writing channel to help human authors to create income and it can also help authors to bring new creative mind and new topic fun content books to let readers to know and buy to read from electronic publisher network platform.

Why does human behavior may be one kind of new human network job to bring global economic advantages.

ALthough, it may be free income or without inocme, but the person does the network behavior, his/her behavior may be bring advantages to influence many other people's health. For this case, when a worker in a coffee shop in an airport gets a vaccination aganinst the flu, it does not only helps him or her stay healthy, but also helps the many travellers who might otherwise have been inflected if that workers caught the flu. So, the externality , the result implies the vaccination of even a part of a community conveys benefits to the whole community. For example, governments pay special attention to the vaccinations of school children, teachers, health mothers, and the elderly, categories of people particularly susceptible not only to catching, but also to transmitting a disease.

It is not accidential that governments are heavily involved with vaccination . When there are externalities, free market, fail to persuade individual incentives with society's

their the worker's decision of whether to get a vaccine ends up attracting whether other people get sick. The workers might not fully take all these other people's potential suffering into account when making her or his vaccination decision.

As Stanford University does many suggestions, understand this and tries to help them make the right decisions and so providers free flu vaccines for its staff and students.

Small pockets of unvaccinated individuals can allow a disease to gain a spread more widely well-being. For example, parent weighing the costs and benefits of a vaccine for their child is not always thinking of the consequences of that vaccination to other people. THese are markets in which subsidizing or regulating behavior can make everyone better off. Because the reason for requiring that a child be vaccinated before enrolling in school is not just to protect that child, because each child's vaccination affects others via potential contagions.

Robots take our jobs behavioral and economy influences

Robot job behavior brings economy influences

If one day robots can replace human to do simple, even complex jobs. They will bring what influences to our global societial economy.The popular economic refrain declares that the

global middle class is dying and robots will soon take our jobs, e.g. shopping center customer service jobs, library service jobs, cinema ticket sale jobs, restaurant kitchen cooker jobs,

even, bus drivers, taxi drivers etc. public transport driving jobs, accountant, doctors etc. professional jobs. Whether it is beautiful or petty matter if our future societies have many human jobs can be replaced to do from robots. Businessman must may reduce to employ employees and reduce to pay salary or wage, when robots can be replaced to do their employees tasks. But, societies must bring unemployement rate rises , due to societies will have many people loss jobs when their employers choose to buy robots to serve their clients or do any office tasks or customer service or cleaning etc. tasks.

In micro economy view, employers may save money in long term, but in macro economy view, it will cause unemployment ratio rises , even crime rate rises when there are many people lose

jobs in societies. These models of doom, though, fail to account for the hundreds of businesses riding the waves of change in their industries when robots may be invented to replace human to do many simple , even complex tasks in our future societies.

WE may image that one small factory needs to manufacture fishes canes to sell to supermarket, the small , cheaper stuff and higher margin parts of the fishes manufacture industry. Before, this factory needs to employe many human factory workers need to help every fresh customer makeing the perfect fishing gear, designed for performance, durability, and cost in order to achieve to manufacture every fish cane in whole fished processing manufacturing stages. Every worker needs to spend about 15 to twenty minutes to finish every fish cane , till to delivery to any supermarket to sell. If this fish canes manufacturing factory can apply manufacturing robots to help them to finish any one working tasks , every robot can only spend five minutes to finish whole fresh fish cane manufacturing process. Thus, every robot can help this factory save 10 to 15 minutes time to finsh every fish cane manufacturing process. IN fact, time is money, because when every robot can help this factory to reduce 10 to 15 minutes time to compare human worker. Then, this factory can finish about 20 fish canes in one hour if it can use robot to help it to manufacture fish canes. Otherwise, if this factory still use human workers to help it to manufacture fish canes, then it can finsh about 3 to 4 fish canes in one hour. SO, the manufacturing efficiency ensures that robots must help this fish manufacturing factory to raise fish canes number more than human workers. So, in robotic behavioral economy view, manufacturing robots must help this fish canes manufacturing factory to raise fish canes manufacturing number and deliver increasing number to supermarkets to prepare to sell every day. Robots can help this fish canes

manufacturing factory bring manufacturing time saving, rising manufacturing efficiency, improving performance and reducing wages expenditure long time advantages in micro economy view. However, manufacturing robots can also bring disadvanages to society, e.g. increasing unemployment ratio, increasing crime rate,
this factory workers will lose jobs and income, they need earn social welfare from government and increasing government finance pressure in short time, even long time in macro economic view.

Stanford University graduate program in economics, Scott lecturer explained that "in demand and supply economic theory for robots supply and demand case, robots supply number increasing may influence human workers demand number decrease. It sometimes calls " the efficient frontier".
No specific human beings were mentioned in any of economics classes. As robots supply and demand in market case, They (robots) may be purely theoretical " agents" who reached to the most reasonable sale prices in order to persuade any one businessman buyer to make manufacturing robot buying decision whether robots can help him / her to bring how much saving time , saving money, saving cost, improving performance, efficiency economic benefit before he/she plans to reduce workers number when he/she decides to apply robots to replace human workers in his/her factory or office or any service department, e.g. cinema ticket sale service, shopping center customer service, shopping center cleaning , supermarket customer service etc. service or sale tasks. When robots can replace human to do any one of these tasks in any organizations. So, robots may be human worker agents who reached to prices the way robots would react to a software

command. There was nothing that explained why some people thrived and others did n't or why truly brilliant, hardworking people could fail when much lazier folks succeeded." Having been admitted to the Stanford University graduate program in economics, Scott lecturer hoped to get his answers there.

How robots influence our future social changing? Using the right technology can be a boon to your business in this economy. For internet example, it is easier than ever to find well-matched customers all around the world, to stay in contact with them, and to more quickly design the products they want. If you focus solely on being cutting -edge, though you risk letting the technology
take over what should be very robust relationships with your customers , employees, and colleagues. IN nowaddays society, technoligical advances and cutomation, personal
relationships in business are more crucial than ever. I mean that robots can not replace human to serve clients to let them to feel more comfortable and passion more easily. For shoe shop case example, if the shoe shop apply one robot to serve its clients to replace human shoe salesperson to serve its shoe customers. Robots ensure that they can not persuade every shoe potential buyer to make shoe buying decision more easily when robots need to contact every shoe potential buyer. The reason is simple, because robots can not touch any one shoe buyer individual emotion very easier.

If the shoe buyer needs the robots to help him/her to choose any right shoe styles when he/she can not feel himself / herself can make the most right shoe style choice decision. The robots can not replace human shoe salesperson to make shoe style choice judgement more easily. They must need longer time to analyze whether which shoe style may be the most suitable to the shoe buyer. Otherwise, human shoe salesperson may attempt to make the most right shoe style choice decision to help any one shoe buyer to chooce the most right style shoe because he/she owns shoe style sale experience, shoe style knowledge, the most important reason is that they can feel every shoe customer individual emotion to touch whether he/she will feel comfortable or happy when they attempt to help every shoe customer to seek the most right shoe style in every shoe customer whole shoe searching processing. Othwerwise, serving robots are only one machine, they can not touch or feel every shoe customer individual emotion whether he/she feel comfortable or unhappy or happy when they need to contact them in whole shoe searching processing. Hence, I believe that some tasks robots can

not repalce human staff to do very easily. Otherwise, robots may bring disadvanatges to let any one businessman to loss his/her customers, due to robots can not touch every customer

emotion to compare human staff in service tasks more easily. Robots serving customer behaviors may cause money lose and customers number lose to the shop in micro economic view.

Intellectual human economic behaviors

What does intellectual human economic behaviors mean ? I believe that when we choose or decide to do intellectual behaviors, then our societies will be influenced to bring economic growth in consequence.I shall attempt to indicate pollution case to explain how and why eithet our intellectual or foolish behaviors may bring economic growth or recession in consequence as below:

On one hand, for air pollution social case aspect example, if we only consider to buy cars to drive for working aimr or holiday leisure aim. Then, our societies air will be polluted. Our health will be influenced to bad. Our car driving behaviors may cause global environment air pollution serously. In long tiem, global air pollution will bring our bodies health to be bad. Although, ourselves car driving behaviors may bring our driving travelling leisure enjoyment and comfortable feeling in short time, also we so not need to pay public transport fare often, but we need to compensate ourselves health economic intangible loss due to air pollution , when cars number increases, dirty air will cause ouselves health to become bad.

In the result, we will need to pay more medical expenditure when we are old age, due to ourselves bodies will become bad, due to we breathe global dirty air every day, due to ourselves cars pollute air in long time, e.g. 10 to 20 years, even 30 more without limited air pollution environment. So, driving cars behavior may be one kind of human foolish behavior and our foolish behavior may bring ourselves future long time medical expenditure absolutely.

One the other hand, water pollution social aspect, if we often keep much rubblish to pollute sea, oil exploration porcessing pollute ocean , ships gas pollute ocaen, then fishes will eat polluted food and drive dirty water, due to global ocean is polluted.

In fact, because human only to conside how to buy boats to carry on leisure enjoyment activities, or catch cruises to travel on the sea. Also, oil manufacturers only consider researching anywhere to find new oil exploration places to manufacture oil product, when their oil exploration processes pollute ocarn . Consequently, global fishes drink polluted warer or eat polluted food. They will have poison. SO, human will have high chance to eat poison polluted fishes, due to fishes are poison or are polluted.

So, human is doing foolish activities, we only hope to find oil exploration places to pollute ocean or we only spend money to buy ticket to catch ships to travel anywhere in global ocean. All of these human foolish behaviors will bring pollution to global ocean. On consequently, we will need to compensate to eat polluted or dirty or poision fishes, ourselves bodies health will be bad. In long time, we need have high chance to pay medical expenditure when we are old. So, pollution case may be one good example to explain how and why human foolish behavior may influence ourselves future need to compensate serious medical loss.

All of these human foolish behavior will bring pollution to global ocean. On consequently, we will need to compensate to eat polluted or dirty or poison fished , ourselves bodies health will be bad. In long time, we will have high chance to pay medical expenditure, when we are old. So, pollution case may be one good example to explain how and why human ourselves intellectual or foolish behaviors may influence future long time economic loss or economic growth or recession in micro and micro economic view.

On another water pollution aspect hand, if we often keep rubbish to sea, oil exploration processing pollutes ocean and ships' gas pollute ocean, then fishes will eat polluted food and drink dirty water, due to fishes will eat polluted food and drink dirty sea water because the global ocean is polluted seriously.

In fact, because human only consider how to buy boats to carry on any leisure water activities, or catches cruises to travel on the sea. Also, oil manufacturers only consider any where to find oil exploratin places to manufacture oil products from ocean, when their pol exploration processes can plooute ocean. Consequently, global fishes drink polluted water or eat direty food. They will have poison. So, human will have high chance to eat poison fishes.

Otherwise, such as pollutin case, it can infuence inflation or deflation. Consequently, the reason indicates supply and demand theory. If air pollution is serious, then we will consider health issue, global cars demand number may be influenced to reduce, when global cars number demand will reduce, global car prices and supply number will need to change to fall down in order to attract or persuade global car consumers choose to make car purchase decision.

Hence, global car manufacture number and car price will be influenced to reduce, due to global air pollution issue. Consequently, deflation will occur because when the country citizen usually does not spend much extra saving money to buy car expensive goods. Money value will be low. Otherwise, if global cair pollution is not serious, human considers to buy cars to enjoy driving leisure lives. So, global car demand is influenced to increase , also global car price will also influenced to increase.

Consequently, gobal human will choose to buy cars to drive. Due to we accept to spend extra saving to buy expensive car goods. Car sale price and supply may be influenced to rise up. Money value is influenced to reduce. Inflation may be influenced, due to global car consumers number increases, we would not have extra money to spend easily. Car expensive goods expenditure influences our spending habit to avoid to make car purchase decision more easily. So, human intellectual or foolish activities may bring inflation or deflation consequency in possible indirectly in macro economic view.

On conclusion, above pollution case explain that how and why human intellectual or foolish economic behaviors may bring inflation or deflation consequency as wll as economic growth or recession consequency as well as any goods demand and supply increasing or decreasing consequency. It implies that human behavior may have indirect relationship to influence any goods demand and supply number to either increase or decrease result as well as any goods price will be influenced to increase or decrease in micro and macro economic view.

The relationship between social change and human behavior

Why does economic changes may influence human individual behavioral change? I shall attempt to indicate shopping behavior and staying at home behavior to explain their case and effect relationsip as below:

Human behavior can be influenced by economic change or economic change can be influenced by human behavior? Why does recession may influence consumers reduce shopping desire? In social recession suitation, it is possible that many people lose jobs suddenly, due to businessmen lose many customers. They need to make decision to reduce employees number in order to continue to keep businesses. Consequently, many firms (organizations) their employees may lose jobs. When they have much time, due to lose jobs, they will feel to avoid to spend too much time and money to go to shopping often. Many losing jobs people, they will often stay at homes.

So, they will reduce time to go to shopping, then non essential products won't their preferable choice purchase products. Hence, recession will change many losing jobs people their shopping or consumption desires to avoid to buy non essential products often . Usually when economic boom, many people have jobs to do because consumers number must increase when many people have jobs to do. Then, many people can accept to spend money to buy non essential products often. Many people feel spend time to go to shopping can satisfy their purchase of any kinds of new products useful psychology or desire. So, recession is one good example to explain it can influence many people do not like often to leave homes to go to shopping easily. Many people like to stay at homes, becaue they feel worry about spending too much shopping time when they leave homes. Their staying home time is one good negative shopping behavior example. So, economic change may influence human individual behavior changes , they have direct cause and efect relationship in behavioral economic view.

May human behavior influence economic change? Is it possible that human behavior may bring the country social economic change in macro economic or micro behavioral economic view ? I shall indicate publishing industry example. Do you feel that if there are many students feel learning is very important when they read many books or many of students feel interesting to read or they have reading new books in habit, then it is possible that the country will have many students like to spend time to go to any book shops to choose the books, they feel that they can help they learn new knowledge. Then the country will increase students number, they often spend time to visit any one book shop every week. Their visiting book shops behavior which may become their habits. So, the country will increase students number, they often spend time to visit book shops. Also, it implies that visiting book shops behaviors may be their behavioral habits.

So, when the country has many students often spend time to visit book shops , their visiting book shops behaviors may help any one book shop to raise books sale chance. So, the country's student individual often visiting book shop behaviors, their habitual visiting book shops behaviors must may assist help any one book shop to increase books sale number absolutely.

Consequently, any one book shop , its books sale bumber must be influenced to increase to increase because the country will have many students like or feel need visit book shops habit in order to choose any suitable books to buy to read at home in order to raise themselves learning effort. When the country has many bok shops often have many students visit their book shops, then their books sale number may be influenced to increase. It explain why student individual visiting book shop behavior may help any one book shop sale number increases also.

How human productive behavior may influence economic development

May any country which citizen behavior assist themselves country development? It is one cause and effect economic question. I mean that if the country itself citicen can not concentrate mind or energy to choose to do one kind of industry in order to let themselves country can bring the most benefit, then whether the counry itself economy can bring the most serious economic benefit. I shall attempt to indicate these countries themselves indistry choice to explain whether these countries themselves citizen productive behavior may help themselves countries to achieve the largest economic benefits. I shall indicate as below:

New Zealand farmer individual wine productive behavior

For New Zealand country example, this country concerns itself effort is foucs on farming agricultural aspect. So, this country has many farmers concentrate on farming agricultural aspect. May New Zealanders choose to spend time to produce different kinds of wines, e.g. wine or red grape wine is for the people are eating meat, or they are eating dinner.

When these New Zealanders their behaviors choose to do farming or agriculture to grow and produce different kinds of taste of white or red grape wine drinking products job. Themselves grape agriculture behavior will influence these New Zealanders themselves, they can learn how to improve different kinds of grape wine drinking products in order to achieve every kinds of white or read grape wines taste improving aim during their white or red grape producing process.

Why can New Zealander every individual white or read grape wine producers improve their white or read grape wine taste more easily? In behavioral economic view, it can explain that why any one New Zealander white or read grape wine producer can be encouraged or excited or persuaded to concentrate nervous and energy and effort to learn how to improve their white or red grape wine products easily.

In fact, New Zealand is one agricultural food export country. It has good natural environment resource , e.g. land, seed to provide any one farmer to produce themselves any kinds of agricultrual food products, e.g. fruit, or wine food products. Because New Zealanders know themselves country has enough natural resource . So, in common, many New Zealanders choose to attempt to do farming agricultural jobs in order to export themselves any kinds of fruit or meat or wine products to overseas or sell to domestic in order to earn profit.

So, when these New Zealand farmers number has been increasing every year. This country farmers will feel themsleves competition between this New Zealand farmers themselves are serious due to they may feel New Zealanders choose to do agriculture businesses in order to export themselves different kinds of farming food to overseas or sell to local to earn profit.

Hence, when many New Zealand farmers feel that farmers number has been increasing every year. They will feel themselves competition is serious. They must need to spend much time and nervous and effort to research what method is the best how to produce the best taste of white or red grape wine products in order to let local or overseas wine buyers to choose to buy his/her producing white or read grpae products to drink.

Hence, in competition psychological view, may influence many New Zealand white or reaad wine producers had been beginning to change their learning behavior on researching what method is the best in order to produce the best quality of taste red or white wine products to sell in order to attract overseas or local white or read grape wine drinkers to choose to buy his/her wine products. Their behavior will focus on learning how to raising or improving white or read grape wine taste method more than only focus on producing a large number white or red grape wine products. They believe wine quality is more important to compare wine producing number. So, New Zealand wine producers themselves wine producers behaviors have been changing on concentrating on researching wine quality method aspect more then wine producing number aspect in behavioral economic view.

America high technological productive behavior

For America example, US is one high technological country, it owns many high technological knowledge talent inventors, e.g. computer science inventors. Hence, US must attract many diferent countries owning high technological computer inventors choose to go to US to develop their computer science profession career. Also, it seems that when many computer science inventors or professions choose to go to US to develop themselves computer science new career. In behavioral economic view, due to their leaving themselves countries choice, which may bring influence themselve country job behaviors need to be changed. They must need to adapt US new live. Because they will forgive their past computer science job. These computer science professionals need to spend time to adapt US new lives. They " past computer science job behaviors" will need to be changed to their new US any computer employer's new computer science job model.

Because their traditional computer science jobs needed to be forgot in their themselves countries. They will feel their old computer science job knowledge and behavior needed to change in order to let their US any one new of computer company employer feels satisfactory to accept their new working behavior in any one US computer organization.

So, on the other hand, many US computer company employer will feel that they must need time to accept any one new overseas computer science professions their working behaviors, their working attitude daily, because these foreign comouter science professional, their past computer working behaviors and working attitude must be different to US domestic computer science professions.

In behavioral economic view, these overseas computer science professions, their working behaviors and attitude must be needed to change in order to adapt any one US new computer company itself domestic or local computer science professional stafs themselves daily working behaviors and attitude because these overseas and local computer science professionals must need to team work together.

In behavioral economic view, it is only one way that foreign computer science professionals must need to change themselves past country traditiona daily working behaviors and attitude in order to cooperate with these US local computer science professionals in teams more easily. Consequently, if these foreign compute science professionals can change their past working behaviors and attitude to let any one US local computer science professional feels to cooperate with them easily in short time. Then, the US computer company itself whole computer professional teams themselves efficiencies will be influenced to raised or improved by the changing past working attitude and working behaviors of these foreign computer science professionals. So, in behavioral economic view, only if US any one computer company hopes itself computer teams themselves efficiency can be raised or improved when it decides to employ foreign computer science professionals and US domestic computer science professionals. They need to work in teams together. They must need to let these foreign computer science professionals to know how to change their working behaviors and attitude to let their domestic computer science professionals feel easy to work together. Then, the US computer company itself whole team efficiency must be rasied or improved easily in short time.

- China share market investing behavior

For China share market example, economic development depends on financial market. Because if many Chinese have interest to invest to carry on shares buying and selling activities in orde to learn how to earn shares interest and share profit when the China shareholder can make decision to sell himself/herself shares in the the high price, then he/she can earn money when he/she can sell the China company's shares in the high sale share price position.

If China has many Chinese like to spend time to carry on investing shares activities. Themselves shares buying and selling behaviors will influence China has many companies can increase fund from many Chinese shareholders in order to have enough money to expand or develop themselves businesses in China in long term.

Consequently, when China can have many Chinese like to attempt to carry on buying and selling shares investing behaviors in China share market. Themselves buying and selling shares behaviors can help many Chinese companies have effort to increase enough money or capital in order to continue to do their businesses in long term absolutely. So, it explains why when many Chinese become shareholders , they can assist China will have many companies continue to develop their businesses if many Chinese like to carry on shares buying and selling investing behaviors in long time in China financial investment market nowadays in behavioral economic view.

Printed by Libri Plureos GmbH in Hamburg, Germany